REFUGEES

*A Family's Search for Freedom
and a Church That Helped Them Find It*

Jeanne Jacoby Smith

Author's Voice Publishing
McPherson, Kansas

Refugees: A Family's Search for Freedom and a Church That Helped Them Find It

By Jeanne Jacoby Smith

Cover illustration by Mary Jacoby Jewell
Cover design by Jan Gilbert Hurst

Published by Author's Voice
www.AuthorsVoicePublishing.com
1315 East Euclid, McPherson, KS 67460
620-245-0009

ISBN: 978-0-9970062-1-6
LCCN: 2016908693

Second edition (first edition, 1979)

Dedication

... to our refugee family, Hanh and Bi, My and Tuan, who taught us to love "the other";

... to Church World Service, the relief agency that made our sponsorship possible;

... to Earl and Billie Kornrumpf, who graciously hosted the Nguyens in their home and introduced them to a new life in America;

... to our faithful members at the Lick Creek Church of the Brethren in Bryan, Ohio, who integrated the Nguyens into our church family;

... and to Richart Fischoff, my family's Jewish friend, who escaped five concentration camps in Hitler's Germany during World War II. He and his wife, Johanna, sensitized me profoundly at the tender age of 13. מהש וכתיי סולשב וחוני. (May they rest in peace.)

Acknowledgments

In addition to the author, many people help in inspiring, advising, encouraging, proofreading, and otherwise helping to bring a book to life. I am grateful to all those who did so for me, especially to:

... members of the Christian Writers' Workshop in Bryan, who encouraged me to write the Nguyens' story to the finish;

... Crystal Zinkiewicz, United Methodist publications director, who advised me to publish our story for churches resettling refugees today;

... Jan Hurst, my loyal editor and publishing assistant, whose expertise was invaluable as she walked me through the complex editorial and production process.

... and last but not least, I lavish my heartfelt gratitude upon my family—Herb, Adam, and MiRan—for their patience as I scribed the Nguyens' story to the finish.

Contents

> "There comes a premonition, a knowing,
> a picture in our minds not of our own,
> but one that is painted for us."
> ...Jeanne Jacoby Smith

Today's Refugee Dilemma

The infant, Jesus, was a refugee. So were Frédéric Chopin and Anne Frank, not to mention, Madeline Albright, Albert Einstein and theologian Paul Tillich. Since our early immigrants landed on Plymouth Rock, refugees from many countries have formed the bedrock of American society.

In 2015, Antonio Guterres, the United Nations' High Commissioner for Refugees, shocked the world with this startling pronouncement: "More people fled last year than at any other time in our records. Around the world, almost 60 million people have been displaced by conflict and persecution. Nearly 20 million are refugees, and more than half are children."[1]

Guterres elucidates: "In 2014, an average of 42,500 people became refugees, asylum-seekers or internally displaced persons, every single day. These people rely on us for their survival and hope. They will remember what we do."[2]

In light of today's global crisis, philanthropic organizations are gearing up for action. Church World Service, Mennonite Central Committee, Lutheran World Relief, Catholic Charities, the National Association of Evangelicals, the International Rescue Committee, and others are preparing to resettle this unprecedented outpouring of humanity.

Though schools may teach us our histories, many lessons we learn from the heart. In this spirit, *Resettling Refugees: A Family's Search for Freedom and a Church That Helped Them Find It* will walk readers through the daily experiences of one family who sought amnesty, and found it.

Using this book as a model, churches will find it a helpful resource for resettling refugees in the 21st century.

Jeanne Jacoby Smith, Ed.D.
McPherson, Kansas

---

[1] "World at War—UNCHR Global Trends: Forced Displacement in 2014"
http://unhcr.org/556725e69.html

---

[2] Ibid. Antonio Guiterres. (20 June 2015). www.unhcr.org/558016eb6.html

1

From Malaysia with Love

Our church's decision to sponsor refugees of war

Our '78 Volaré defied the upcoming storm as it sped through the Ohio countryside. Lightning flashed in the distance while puddles spattered our muddy sedan, the second in a caravan. Herb's foot loitered from the throttle momentarily while the lead car slowed, then picked up speed again. Whisking wheels on the slippery dark highway sprayed the car in the rear.

I slid down deep into the back seat, my mind in a whirl. Was this November of 1975, or April of 1979? The November emotions replicated themselves in this new April experience. Three years previously, we had traveled on an evening like this to New York City to welcome MiRan, our infant daughter from Korea. And now, we were headed for the airport in Toledo, Ohio, and within minutes of adopting an entire family.

I closed my eyes to restrain hot tears. *Tonight we'll be launching a new life for these people. What kind of hell did they experience in Vietnam? What will be their emotions?*

We yearned to know but shuddered at their possible answers, for if something happens once in history, can it not happen again?

Only months before, it seemed like days, our church had wrestled with the issues. The refugees' faces stared at us from newspapers and the television. "Hungry, helpless, and homeless" were the anchorman's choice of words.

Thousands dangled from the spider web of fate, people without a country, with nowhere to call home. We, the free peoples of the world, appeared as gods at the top with power, either to save them or to walk away and let their wretched souls fade into oblivion. The story of yet another vessel overcrowded with desperate people and capsizing in the South China Sea had become an all too frequent feature of our nightly newscasts.

As a church with the commission to "welcome the stranger,"[3] we felt a responsibility to do all we could, given their hopeless situation.

---

[3]Leviticus 19:34; Matthew 5: 43-44; Matthew 25: 35-40; John 4: 7-30; Hebrews 13: 1

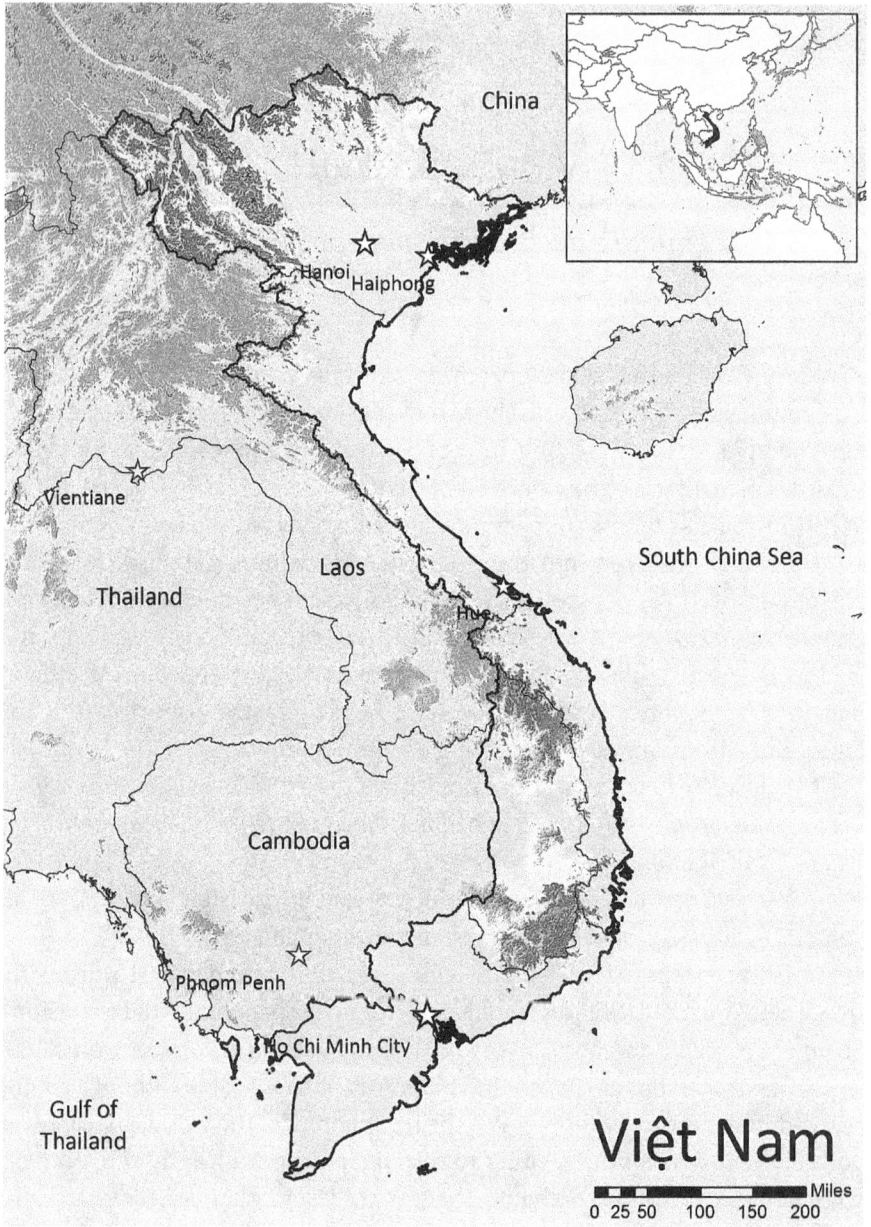

China

Hanoi
Haiphong

Vientiane

Laos

Thailand

Hue

South China Sea

Cambodia

Phnom Penh

Ho Chi Minh City

Gulf of
Thailand

Việt Nam

Miles

0 25 50   100   150   200

2
"Chao"

The only verbal link between our worlds—I had to say it.

The whistling hums of jets roared in the background, blurring our voices inside the airport. Dr. Trinh nodded his head politely. "You may call me 'Chung'," his controlled voice modulated.

Earl and Billie sought long and hard to find an interpreter for our family. Excitement over the family's arrival did not drain their enthusiasm but, rather, spurred it on.

They found Chung in a matter of days. In Vietnam, he had worked as a veterinarian, but during the war, he was employed by the Americans. Resettled by United Methodists in Bryan, he was fluent in English and agreed to be the translator for our family.

Earl swung his lanky body around to introduce our group. Of Louisiana heritage, he sported a mild but authoritative manner. He and Billie had met in the military when they were stationed in Jacksonville, Florida. They prided themselves in their ecumenical wedding long before the ecumenical movement began. Earl, a Roman Catholic, married Billie, a Methodist, with a Catholic priest officiating. A Jewish friend played the organ and a Lutheran ushered while his Baptist buddy gave away the bride. And now, the couple was actively involved in the Church of the Brethren, a small, Anabaptist denomination rooted in New Testament pacifism.

Billie, a young boisterous WAVE at the time, boasted the distinction of being the only woman on base who could look a six-foot soldier straight in the eye. Yet her height did not restrain her loving manner. In fact, Billie's middle name was 'Love'. She bubbled with it, reflected it in her laughter and lavished it on everybody just as she planned to do with the family now.

"Chung," Earl announced, with a gesture of his hand, "this is our friend, Florence. She will be the English teacher for the husband."

Florence acknowledged Chung's greeting, and he bobbed his head politely.

3

". . .and this is Wilma, the teacher for your wife."

In her unhesitant manner, Wilma stepped forward and thrust her hand aggressively toward him. Flashing a smile in his direction, she nodded and said, "Glad to meet you, Mr. Chung"

Everybody liked Wilma in spite of her occasional brashness. After the veneer of social graces wore away, usually in the first minute or two, Wilma became her honest self. . .audacious, quick-witted, and forthright. The fact that she had served in Nigeria as a missionary and had a global consciousness endeared her to us more.

Chung acknowledged Wilma's greeting.

Earl proceeded to introduce my husband, Herb, who grasped Hanh's hand and shook it.

MiRan snuggled her miniature body against her daddy's leg and smiled bashfully at the little newcomers. Her black hair and almond eyes gave away her identity.

Hanh receded slightly, and I wondered what he was thinking. . .'Do Americans steal refugee children? Where is this little girl's mother?'

Bi wanted to react, but her reticent spirit shied away from responding.

Chung hesitated, and then mustered up the courage. "May I ask where your daughter was born?"

Herb lifted the wiggling angel up in his arms. "South Korea," he said. "We adopted her as a baby."

We always spoke affectionately of MiRan's adoption, convinced that openness and honesty would enhance her self esteem in years to come. Chung seemed pleased that we chose to internalize part of his Asian culture with our own.

I slipped my arms around Adam's shoulder and pulled him to my side. Strangers often asked about MiRan, but seldom attended to him. Adam needed assurance that he was important, too.

"And this is her brother, Adam," I said.

Adam stood proud and said, "An' she's my little sister!"

—◄o►—

Earl interrupted our formalities, eager to get on with business.

"Mr. Chung," he said politely, "can you tell us what to expect. . .information about the Vietnamese culture that will help us understand them? How can we make them happy?"

"Ah," Chung complied stoically. "Your request is proper and natural,

4

but in Vietnam we do not seek happiness. In America everybody try to be happy. In Vietnam, we seek peace of mind."

The words burst in small puffs from Chung's lips. Though our vocabulary was second nature to him, the English language persisted in guttural spurts of air unlike his native tongue.

"I understand your sentiments," he said, then added, "What else might you wish to know?"

Not knowing what else to ask of him, the conversation deteriorated as we broke into conversation with each other.

◄o►

Wilma leaned over my shoulder and brushed my arm, her mind on another matter. She enunciated her thoughts in a loud stage whisper.

"We're missing 'Jesus of Nazareth' tonight. . .the TV special," she said.

Florence leaped from her seat, accosting Wilma's inclination. "But this where I want to be."

Wilma stiffened in self-defense. "But I wouldn't have come if I didn't want to be here," she snapped. The two teachers had a ambiguous relationship, and I usually kept my distance when they fussed with each other. But Easter was approaching, and Wilma's analogy was all too pertinent.

"Ladies," I swallowed, "we're going to meet Jesus of Nazareth personally tonight. . .right here!"

Wilma relaxed. "You're right," she said.

Florence agreed, and then was distracted by Chung who wanted to work on our language lessons.

"*Chao. . .chao ba,*" he enunciated meticulously, "means 'hello' to the woman."

We stiffened to attention. "*Chao ba,*" we repeated in unison, floundering as we tried to imitate his cadences.

". . .and *chao ong*. . .you must say to the man," he continued.

"*Chao–awwng,*" we slurred together.

"No! *Chao-ong, chao-ong,* like in 'long,'" Wilma insisted.

Her ability to replicate Chung's inflections almost dizzied me.

"T'ank you," Chung replied, grateful for her assistance. "And *chao co* is for little children. You can say?"

"*Chao co-o-o,*" we droned, obliging our tutor with perfect intonations.

Earl scratched his head. "What is it for the man again?"

"*Chao ong.*"

"Oh, I thought that was for the woman," someone said.

"Me, too," another concurred.

"What's the word for the children again?" Billie asked.

The many forms of 'chao' bewildered us. One greeting was used for a superior, another for a minor, and even they differed depending upon the sex of the person addressed.

"Please, Chung, there's got to be a simpler way," Billie laughed, overwhelmed by our semantic shenanigans.

"A crash course in 'chao-ology' won't do it for us now," I muttered.

Chung perked his ears at 'chao-ology'. My makeshift word was not part of his repertoire.

"Chao," he replied, ignoring my remark. "Just say 'Chao.' They'll understand."

The respected doctor tilted his head to change the subject. "May I ask where they are coming from?"

"Someplace in Vietnam," Herb offered. "That's all we know right now."

<o>

My fascination with Chung's mannerisms made me wonder where he came from. Vietnam, of course, but what precipitated his departure? He was here in Bryan alone. After four long years in exile, perhaps he could tell us about it.

"Do you have a family, Chung?"

Chung's eyes dropped and he fell silent.

Immediately, I realized that I had infringed on a very private aspect of his life. I cringed, searching uncomfortably for a way out. My face worked nervously as everyone's eyes focused in my direction. I wanted to swallow my words and forget them, but it was too late.

When I met Chung's gaze, I saw that I had impinged on a tender spot . . . a secret too painful to risk with the world. Little did we know then what time would eventually reveal to us. . .that Chung left a wife and son in that god-forsaken land to which he could never return.

Billie tried to salvage me. "Maybe he'd rather not talk now," she said.

<o>

Chung sat quietly, as if in meditation. Internally, he screamed defiance at his fate, but outwardly he appeared placid and calm—like a meditating Buddha, minus its contented smile. I examined his stoic eyelids, pupils receding beneath them, looking back into time, far back to another country, another land. There the sleek figure of a refined woman waved in the distance. A year-old toddler tugged at its mother's *ao dai*, the flowing tunic draped around her body. Her voice called out to him, "See you on the weekend, honorable husband!"

But the weekend never came, for a day en-route to Tay Ninh, distressing news flooded the airwaves. South Vietnam was under siege and falling to the North. It was only a matter of days. His countrymen, and the Americans, must take departure immediately. Already, swarms were crowding the airports, awaiting evacuation. 'Bloodbath' was the word. It battered their furrowed brows.

The friend who was driving stopped. "What shall we do?" he said, looking to Chung for wisdom.

Chung could not speak for the obstruction in his throat.

The friend continued. "We cannot return home. We must go the shortest route and leave the country."

Chung squared his shoulders. His face took on a languid color as he searched for answers. He did not want to make that horrendous decision, so he waited for his friend to make it for him. But the truth was evident.

"Drive South to Saigon, Mr. Ming, drive south," Chung sighed, leaning his weary head against the headrest.

He knew what North Vietnam did to its enemies. He had seen them massacre his villagers. Nobody was innocent. If they caught you in their path, you were guilty and you died. Silently, he prayed his family would escape. Prospects would be better if he were not there to jeopardize them.

Chung had worked in Vietnam as a veterinarian for Americans. Continuing toward the airport, he and Ming boarded a plane headed for Chicago.

Hours later, he would never forget how his body shivered when the voice of his friend broke the concentrated silence. "We'll be in America soon, Chung. We'll be landing soon."

—◄○►—

Billie looked at her watch, and her musical voice glided Chung back to reality. "Only a few more minutes! They'll be in Toledo soon!"

Chung's American friends from Bryan chattered endlessly about subjects of little interest to him, but it would be good to see countrymen again and hear the language of his people.

Earl's eyes darted restlessly at his watch. Leaning back in his chair, he crossed his arms like a toy fireman ready to drive his iron horses into the scene of action.

Billie paced the floor like an expectant mother. MiRan and Adam tried to sleep in a pile of coats, to no avail. Each time the PA system made another announcement, they hopped from their makeshift beds and chased each other mercilessly around posts in the airport.

—◄o►—

We waited. And we waited. We were not good at waiting. I didn't know anyone who was.

Secretly, I wondered how we would look to the family. Big? Tall? Pale-faced? Some of us overweight? Would our splendid cars and dazzling lights be a mockery to the simple life they cherished?

After midnight a supersonic jet droned down the runway, let out a grinding roar, then inched toward the terminal and powered down. Passengers processed to the concourse, one by one.

A few minutes later, a young mother with black sleek hair and slanted eyes appeared with a wide-eyed little boy in her arms. She sauntered across the carpet, then stopped and waited, alone. I could not discern whether the child clung to his mother, or the mother to the child.

Chung hesitated to address her. Protocol dictated that he speak with the husband first.

Moments later, her husband exited the plane with a young girl-child clinging to his hand. His cheeks were taut, his eyes naked with hope. This was an anxious moment for his family.

Chung hesitated, then approached and greeted them. They conversed for several minutes.

—◄o►—

There they were . . . 'Jesus of Nazareth', in the form of a frightened family. They appeared small and alone, in a strange world. All their worldly possessions the father carried in one duffle bag. The children appeared to have no coats.

Chung, our indispensible middle-man, told us they had been traveling for two days and they were very tired. "Days and nights," he said, "are opposite in Malaysia."[4] We, also, learned that Bi, the mother, had lost a child in her third trimester of pregnancy. Neither of the parents had any command of English.

---

[4] In the U.S. Eastern Standard Time is 12 hours later.

Dr. Chung, filtered our questions through the cargo of his knowledge as he translated.

"Will we have language teachers?" They intoned through Chung.

Chung singled Wilma and Florence out from the group. They nodded their heads politely. He spoke a few more words, and then drew Billie and Earl aside to explain their living arrangement with the Kornrumpfs.

My husband, Herb, the pastor of our church, seemed simple enough to explain, but their concept of 'church' was non-existent. However, they were very respectful and nodded in appreciation.

Glancing at our group, Chung realized he excluded one person during his introductions . . . me.

What could he say about me? I wasn't a teacher. Nor was I a host. So, who was I?

"I'm just a friend, Chung. Tell them I'm their friend."

I looked at the family and opened my mouth to greet them. My lips were dry, and the words stuck in my throat, but that one word was the only verbal link between our worlds, and I had to say it.

"*Chao*," I managed to whisper.

Florence choked, "*Ch, chao.*"

Even Wilma . . . Wilma who never lacked for words . . . nodded her head and managed a raspy, "*Chao.*"

The presence of Jesus was very real in those moments.

We were standing on holy ground.

Billie fumbled awkwardly in her bag. Somewhere in the jumble were two stuffed animals for the children, a welcome to America.

"Chung, give these to the little ones. They're afraid of me."

My's dark eyes darted from the animal to her mother. She hesitated to accept it. Tuan turned his back, afraid. Bi reassured the children, and their tiny arms encircled the balls of fur from the white-haired grandma. Hanh relaxed into a smile, and Bi looked pleased.

Earl offered the family the warm coats we brought, which they gladly accepted. The time had come to leave.

—◦—

As we processed through the terminal, I glanced at them again. Petite My ran alongside her father in her rubber sandals. I had spent the afternoon replacing black fur with white on MiRan's outgrown winter coat, but style meant little now for it hung loosely on My's frail body. Little Tuan clung tenaciously to his mother. Bi traipsed alongside Hanh wearing my old gray coat, the one I used for yard chores. It hurt me to think I almost threw it away, but it pained me more that I didn't give her my best.

Little did we know that behind those trembling hearts lay a more traumatic experience than this one, for we learned in days to come that our family, indeed, had experienced the pain of the cross.

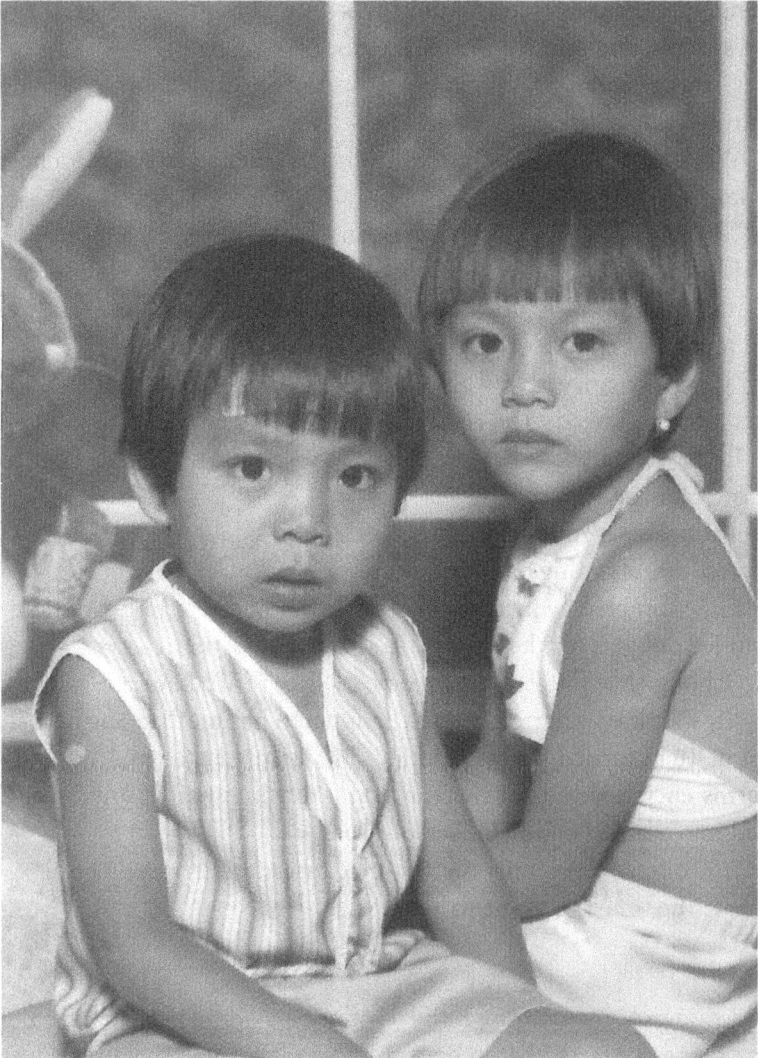

Siblings Tuan and My Nguyen at the Toledo airport

3
"First Daze"

Culture Shock

"Earl, they're sleeping in their clothes," Billie whispered as she closed the door behind her.

At 2:00 a.m. she finally stood in the hallway and bid the family goodnight. Before she turned to leave, she watched Hanh throw back the covers and crawl in, fully clothed.

Startled at his behavior, Billie blurted, "Hanh, what are you doing?"

As expected, he didn't understand. While he studied Billie's astonished face, Bi promptly lifted the blankets on her side of the bed and slipped in, also in full attire.

"Earl," Billie shook her head in frustration, "I purposely bought pajamas for them. I laid them across the bed so they'd know what they were." Exasperated, she struggled to sort out the pieces. But where to begin? There must be some logical way to explain 'pajamas' to non-English speakers.

'Simplify, Billie,' she said to herself. 'Simplify everything.'

—◀○▶—

The Kornumpf home, indeed, struck the family as extravagant. When they left the house and returned, they would step inside, glance from one elegant furnishing to another, and then, promptly remove their shoes before treading lightly across the carpet.

The Kornrumpfs' sofa sat primly in the living room amidst heart-shaped philodendrons. Portraits on the wall eyed them from brass frames, while raindrops dripped from a graceful Grecian statue in the alcove near the hall. Rich mahogany cupboards, the copper-tone refrigerator, and chrome-laden microwave all but jumped from their assigned stations and screamed, 'Look at me!' And the strange brown box under the counter that washed the dishes without their help was beyond their wildest dreams. Never had they experienced a kitchen with more than the barest essentials.

11

This world was strange, to be sure, creating cultural shock waves for the family. Rather than adapting to natural elements like they did over in Vietnam, a rectangular fixture on the wall manipulated the weather inside. They pushed a button on a box to watch tiny people from far away dance and sing. This was a world with a guttural, frothy language where people drove automobiles rather than bicycles. It was, also, a world of ... *bathrooms!*

Bathrooms? The very first night Billie steered Bi into the bathroom. The children followed their mother into the small enclave, permeated with the fresh scent of lavender and clean towels.

Billie turned the faucet on at the sink, then, splattered the water. "You see, Bi? Water! Water!"

As Bi gently undressed the children for the bath, Tuan slowly inched closer to his mother, fearful of this white-haired lady who jabbered nonsense. When Billie twisted the spigot at the tub and invited him to get in, the water gushed wildly, and Tuan darted from the room as fast as his naked little carcass could carry him.

Bi found him curled on Hanh's lap out in the living room, trembling. She bundled him into her arms and returned to the bathroom obediently.

Billie glanced up. "Come here, Bi!" She grasped Bi's hand and tugged her gently toward the water.

"Hot, hot!"

Splashing a bit on Bi's golden skin, Billie repeated 'hot', watching Bi's eyes for understanding.

Bi flinched, and then, she nodded.

Billie plopped the child into the waiting tub. Tuan panicked.

Letting out a shriek that seemed more than the sum of his meager little parts, he screamed at full lung power while scrambling to escape the sudsy water. Bi tried to restrain his slippery body while Billie struggled frantically to wash the flailing arms and legs.

Four-year-old My watched, then acquiesced to the ordeal more stoically. She didn't cry or smile.

Finally, the bath was over. With outstretched arms the matriarchs carried their dripping carcasses, kicking, into the bedroom where they were swaddled in stiffly creased pajamas.

The matriarchs tucked them in and saw them off to sleep.

◄○►

Billie guided Bi back to the bathroom.

"Bi," she said, motioning toward the tub, "it's your turn now."

When Bi appeared puzzled, Billie unbuttoned her own blouse to model the desired behavior. Waving her hand toward the tub, she said, "You, you, Bi!"

As Bi began to undress, Billie started fresh water. Flopping a fluffy towel across the counter, she left the room.

Minutes later, Bi emerged and positioned herself next to her husband on the sofa. She had obeyed the coiffured lady, but instead of donning the newly purchased nightgown, she dressed again in her musty clothes, the ones she wore all the way from Malaysia.

Billie caught Earl's eye and shot him a rueful smile. He grinned back vaguely, and then, realized they could talk without restraint since the family didn't know English.

"Don't worry, honey," he yawned. "They'll dress for bed when they get to their room."

"I hope so," Billie added wistfully. "But now it's your turn to help Hanh with the bath. It's awfully late. I'm tired."

". . . and I have to work tomorrow," Earl added. He lifted his body wearily from the chair to repeat the bathroom sequence.

"Come, Hanh! Your turn!"

Hanh rose and followed him like a puppy, but as quickly as Earl turned the corner, Hanh did an about-face and retreated.

Earl swirled around on his heels. "No, Hanh, you go here!" Daddy America grasped his ruffled shoulder and pointed to the bathroom.

Hanh peered imploringly at Bi, spewed a long string of Vietnamese, then shook his head vigorously, and returned his gaze to Earl.

He wagged his head . . . '*No!*'

Earl slipped his hand from Hanh's shoulder and looked at Billie. "We can't force him to take a bath, can we?"

Secretly, he hoped she'd agree.

"No," she conceded. Honoring Hanh's wishes was more important.

◄◦►

The early morning light haloed Earl's lanky silhouette, stretching his shadow toward the ceiling and filling the room. He slowly pushed the door aside, exposing a yawning black corridor that led to the family room.

Earl tiptoed discreetly down the hallway toward the bathroom. Thinking he heard a shuffle, he glanced toward the kitchen.

Instantly, the fatigue washed out of him. There in a huddle sat the entire family, all four, in one indivisible whole. They had been awake for hours.

Little My was ill. She had vomited several times during the night, but neither parent had the courage to wake up Billie and Earl.

Earl slipped back to the bedroom. "Honey?" he whispered.

Billie squinted her eyes, then remembered they weren't alone. The anguished expression on Earl's face told her something was wrong.

"We have a problem. My is sick."

Billie threw on her housecoat and padded down the hall. Rubbing the sleep from her eyes, she knelt beside the little girl.

Gently, she touched My's forehead. She was pale, listless, and burning with fever.

Hanh and Bi's eyes followed Billie as she ran to the bathroom for medicine and a basin of tepid water. Together, they bathed My's scant little body until the blush began to pinken.

By seven a.m., Billie could wait no longer. "Jeanne," she cried into the phone, "My is sick. She needs a doctor!"

I tucked the English-Vietnamese phrase book under my arm before we all left the house. Herb drove.

When we arrived at the Kornrumpfs, Bi's face lit up. She recognized me from the airport the night before.

Billie stepped between us. "Our pastor here is . . . Herb. Herb," she enunciated.

"Hub, Hub," Hanh imitated her lip movements. Bi mouthed Herb's name silently and smiled.

"Herb is leader of our church people," Billie continued.

Hanh shook his head and laughed awkwardly.

"Church . . . 'church people' . . . I told you about them," Billie repeated.

But what was 'church people'? They tried so hard to understand.

Hanh clammed up, and I surmised what he was thinking about our daughter, MiRan. *Do Americans steal refugee children? Where is this little girl's mother?* Bi wanted to react, but her reticent spirit shied away from responding.

Billie sensed our dilemma. "Earl, where's the Vietnamese dictionary?" Billie asked, trying to remember.

I approached My while Billie and Earl launched an all out search for the dictionary.

"Is My sick?" I asked, laying my hand on her brow.

Bi's face softened at my concern. She nodded.

When Billie returned, she leaped through the dictionary, surveying its pages briskly. "Adoption," she muttered and showed the word to them.

Left to right: Tuan Nguyen, MiRan Smith, and My Nguyen, with Adam Smith in the back.

A sudden shine came into their eyes.

"Vietnam?" Hanh asked.

Herb wagged his head 'no'. "She's from Korea," he said.

Immediately, the family warmed to us like trembling hands take to a cozy fire, and Bi wrapped our daughter in her arms and hugged her hard. Our little Asian orchid seemed a touch of home for them.

Hanh and Bi chatted in Vietnamese in the back seat with musical intonations. Vowels blended into each other between perfectly positioned lips. The language seemed a language to be sung instead of spoken. I liked it.

"Herb?" I reached out toward him. He glanced at me and read my eyes, then grasped my waiting hand with his.

"We're chauffeuring the world in our car this morning." My hand felt small and fragile, as helpless as a child's in his large but expressive hand.

He chuckled at my sentiments and looked perceptively at me. Something of intangible beauty was happening here, and we were the lucky recipients.

—◄o►—

Glaring eyes followed us down the corridor at the medical center. They scanned the family several times, and then lit upon us. It seemed that eyes were popping from the walls. Expressions ranged from smiles to scowls.

Herb and I had talked of prejudice, but never had it come this close before. Still, we held our heads high for the sake of the family. No apologies were in order. We would not accept less than human treatment due anyone to whom God gave the precious gift of humanity.

Within minutes, we escaped into the sanctuary provided by the doctor's office. The physician, a humble man of middle age, inquisitively looked at Herb and me. "How are we going to do this?" he chuckled.

I laughed nervously. "We brought a phrase book, Dr. Moats. We'll point to words and parts of the body. I hope that helps." I prudently glanced at Herb. I could hear him talking inside my head. *Sure, Jeanne, you go right ahead and I'll watch.*

Dr. Moats sat My on the table and very tenderly did what he had to do. She flinched, but did not cry, looking continually toward her parents for reassurance.

The three-way conversation began. "Does she have a fever," the doctor asked.

My fingers flew quickly down the page. "*Toi bi sot* — I have a fever." I pointed to the sentence and tried to pronounce it. My Vietnamese was pitiful.

Herb couldn't resist trying. This was a mental game. He placed his hand on his forehead and pointed to My's.

"My . . . *Toi bi sot?*" he asked.

Bi nodded her head. I looked to Dr. Moats. "She does."

The doctor probed My's tiny abdomen. "What about her stomach? Does it hurt?"

My fingers slipped down the column again, across the long list of body terms. "Ribs, spine, stomach . . . Here it is!" Pointing to the word, 'bung,' the doctor asked, "Hurt?"

Herb interrupted. "They don't understand 'hurt.' Let me do it, doctor."

Herb wrapped his arms around his abdomen and exhaled a grueling "Oh-h-h-h!" Bi and Hanh grinned at the crazy guy and nodded, 'yes.'

We looked at Dr. Moats. He was laughing, too. "It hurts," we said together.

"Diarrhea?" Dr. Moats continued, sitting on the corner of his desk now. We soared down the list of medical ailments. "Malaria . . .

cholera . . . typhoid. Searching for their equivalents in Vietnamese, I tried to pronounce the words with Bi and Hanh looking over my shoulder. We were communicating through "The Book."

Hanh caught Bi's eye and asked her something, to which she retorted with assonant intonations. Their eyes darted from each other and back to the printed page. They read it again, and then, answered 'No.'

The doctor resumed the examination, patiently taking My step by step through the medical regimen. The diagnosis? Malnutrition and an upset stomach from strange food and the reversal of day and night.

No wonder the little girl had problems. Her familiar world of rice gruel and thatched huts made an irrevocable turnabout, in a mere forty-eight hours, to a strange land laden with tables of rich food and homes of cushioned floors. 'No food' became too much food. 'Nothing' became Everything. Her schema was topsy-turvy, her world turned upside down.

─◄o►─

We took My home that morning, all of us relieved. Her problems were not yet resolved, but at least we knew where the struggle lay. Billie tackled that struggle with all her heart in the days that followed.

Before we left, I found a phrase in The Book that expressed what I wanted to say to them.

"*Khong co sao dau,*" I struggled.

Hanh and Bi stepped quickly to my side, peered over my shoulder, and smiled.

"Everything will be all right," The Book elucidated.

Bi moved near me as I opened the door.

I didn't know what she wanted, but Billie knew. "She wants to hug you, Jeanne."

I looked at Bi and opened my arms.

We embraced for one brief moment. She accepted my friendship, and I felt blessed.

Left to right: My, Bi, Hahn, and Tuan Nguyen

4
First Week...or Weak?

Building Relationships

An amused expression played at the corners of Billie's mouth as she tightly tied the sash of her long robe around her waist and walked out to the living room.

Earl looked up from the evening paper. "What's the matter, honey? Are you OK?" Holding his watch at a measured distance, he added, "It's only six o'clock."

"Pajamas!" Billie exclaimed. "I'm throwing propriety to the wind. I'll teach them by example!"

Earl knew his wife was clever, but this was downright cunning. "I'll do the same," he said, dropping the newspaper beside his Lazy Boy.

Shortly, Earl appeared in pajamas and bathrobe. Hanh inspected him curiously.

"We wear these to bed in America, Hanh," he said. Earl modeled the loose-fitting apparel and scuffed around the living room the remainder of the evening.

"Come!" Billie motioned for Bi to follow. She steered the children toward the bathroom with Bi following. Billie's grandmotherly instinct won the children's hearts this night by smothering them in bubbles.

Feeling better now, My crawled on top of the toilet seat. Facing the wall, she curled her toes around the rim.

"Bi, what on earth is she doing?" Billie blurted, certain the child would tumble into the water.

Bi barked a command to My, who retorted with a sense of urgency. Before Billie could scamper across the floor, My pushed down her slacks and squatted. It was too late.

Bewildered at the child's behavior, Grandma "Ame'dica" burst into laughter.

Bi was thoroughly confused, not knowing what caused her laughter.

19

After the little one finished, Billie grasped her under the arms and tried to lift her, but her toes clung tenaciously to the rim of the seat, which rose upward with her.

"Come on, honey!" Billie coaxed.

Her second attempt was more successful. This time Billie swooshed My's body into the air, switched her around and plopped her on the seat, face frontwards.

Billie bobbed her head toward Bi. "This is how to do it. You will tell the children?"

Bi rattled something to My, but instincts are tenacious. Several times during the ensuing week Billie entered the bathroom, only to find tiny footprints on the toilet seat.

◄o►

That Friday, Hanh and Bi settled into the sofa, prepared to study The Book. They habitually repeated the names, 'Billie' and 'Earl', but the 'll' in 'Billie' and 'rl' in 'Earl' proved too difficult to articulate. Their mouths emitted sounds subtly different from their counterparts in English.

Hanh focused on his hosts. "Heah," he enunciated slowly, "come heah!"

Hanh pointed his index finger at the dictionary. 'Me' . . . 'mother,' it said.

He bunched his wife and daughter together. "Me and My," he repeated.

"We say 'mother and daughter,'" Billie articulated.

Confused, Hanh's face told her the sentence was cluttered with excess words.

Billie pointed toward their daughter, My. "Daughter," she simply said. Then she nodded at Bi and said, "Mommy!"

Hanh took the dictionary and located the word, '*cha.*' Earl removed his bifocals to read the definition. Hanh pointed to himself, then to Tuan and back again. "*Cha,*" he parroted.

"We say 'father' or 'daddy,'" Earl explained.

"Da-dee," Hanh repeated.

Bi mouthed the word silently to herself.

"Hanh . . . Da-dee, Tuan," Hanh said proudly, discovering a new identity. He waved his arm toward Earl and held it there. "You," he faltered, "you, Da-dee Ame'dica."

Billie's cheeks flushed. "He wants to call you Daddy, Earl . . . his American Daddy!"

Deeply moved, Earl slipped his arm around Hanh's shoulder. "Tuan is Hanh's son. Hanh is Daddy's son." Earl punched three fingers into the air. "Son, number three."

Bi withdrew, as if neglected. "Mommy Ame'dica, Mommy Ame'dica," she said, trying to piece her new world together. Color tinged her cool pale cheeks. She lowered her head.

Billie gently caught her in her arms. "Bi, you're my daughter, too."

Earl and Billie Kornrumpf (center) did a stellar job of hosting Hanh (left) and Bi (right)
Nguyen. The Nguyens called them Daddy and Mommy Ame'dica.
(Photo taken at Moore's Pond near Bryan, Ohio.)

◄o►

Hanh and Bi conferred the Kornrumpfs respect due parents in Vietnam. Every evening Bi perused the Kornrumf's photo albums, constructing mental schema for her new life in America.

Peering at the photos, the couple chattered loudly, first about one, and then, another.

"Mommy! Mommy Ame'dica!" Bi called from the living room.

Billie mopped her hands on her apron, glancing in from the kitchen.

Her English became increasingly choppy as she communicated with the family. That wasn't the best approach, she knew, but, at least, they understood her. "What you want, Bi?" she asked.

The couple assimilated phrases quickly, and when a new one added itself to their vocabulary, she relied upon it heavily. She reminded herself continually, "Simplify, Billie. Simplify."

"Come heah," Bi insisted. Billie shuffled to her side.

Hanh pointed to an ageing black and white photo. "Billie . . . Mommy, Da-dee?" he asked.

"Yes, Hanh."

Remorse crept over his face. "Hanh's Mommy, Da-dee, Vietnam," he stated sadly.

Billie hesitated, fearful of conjuring up specters, but they initiated the conversation, so she saw it as an opportunity. She smoothed her apron in place, then cleared her throat and said, "Why Hanh's Mommy, Daddy not in America?"

"Hanh Mommy, Da-dee, no mo-ney. Bi Mommy, Da-dee, same-same."

Billie pressed them. "So how did you come to America if you had no money?"

Hanh pulled out The Book and poked a brown finger to a string of hieroglyphs in Vietnamese.

"'Uncle'. He's pointing to the word, 'uncle,'" Earl said, holding The Book aloft to read it from a distance.

Hanh continued. "Uncle have money . . . " He could not complete his thought for the lack of words. Quickly he paged through The Book again and pointed – "thousand." Hanh lifted four fingers.

"Four thousand . . . dollars?" Earl asked in his distinctive Louisiana accent.

"Yeah," Hanh asserted. "Four t'ousand dollahs."

Through long and tedious discourse Billie and Earl excerpted from their rudimentary conversations that Hanh had lived with his uncle from the age of seventeen. Wealthy by Vietnamese standards, his uncle owned a plantation—one hundred fifty banana trees, fields of onions and tomatoes, and acreage of cabbage. Hanh and Bi tended the farm six months of the year while his uncle operated a business in Can Thau five miles to the south.

When Uncle's land was confiscated during the North's invasion, soldiers hewed down their trees and stripped his family of their livelihood.

Later in camp, only a small garden was allotted each household, barely enough to feed them.

Anger and resentment escalated as the people suffered at the hands of their oppressors. Restlessness pervaded the countryside. The day soon came when the man in Hanh overreached his grasp and he rebelled as other men had done. But his resistance had dire consequences, and he was compelled to go into hiding.

The North, suspecting his family knew more of his whereabouts than they dared to admit, quickly widened the search to include his wife and children. That's when Uncle paid their way.

"How many people were on your boat, Hanh?"

Again, he delved into The Book.

"Eighty . . . and one," Earl clarified, as his surrogate son pointed to the answer.

Hanh cleared his throat. "Malaysia . . . Hanh 'n' Bi cannot come Malaysia." He poked his fingers upward to indicate two times. "Time number t'ree we come Malaysia. Boat no good in water."

He pointed to Bi's back and tied an imaginary sling around her chest. "Tuan . . . here," and as he tightened another around himself, he added, "My . . . here!"

Piecing together the puzzle of their story, Billie gasped an audible "No!" as their troubled world, strangely remote until this moment, came crashing down upon her.

Hanh clawed his arms into the air in swimming motions. "Hanh, Bi, do this, this, this!"

Billie caught her breath. "Earl, their boat was sinking. He said, 'boat no good.'"

Laboriously, detail for detail, Earl and Billie struggled to understand the details of their story.

◄○►

After days of piecing the Nguyen's experience together, Billie and Earl finally concluded that what they surmised was true: As their boat sailed cautiously around the Malaysian peninsula on that sweltering day in July of 1978, their unseaworthy flotsam, filled with human hearts, lunged unknowingly into treacherous shoals veiled by breaking waves, crashing the stern to bits.

Hanh and Bi, and others with them, wagered their strength against imponderable odds. They swam to shore with their children lashed to their backs.

The swelter of water lapping against their bodies obscured their vision of what was happening behind them, for minutes later, their vessel slipped down a slope so steep that it led to the bowels of the ocean.

Of the eighty passengers on board, only ten survived, and they were among the ten.

Billie felt dizzy after hearing the family's horrors. Wrapping her arms around Bi, who bit her lower lip, they wept together, reliving those terrible moments. Hanh sat stoically, his head bowed low, while Earl massaged the tension in his back, finally in touch with the core of Hanh's wretched being.

◄o►

The whisper of dawn gave way to sunshine. As summer approached, it slipped high above the trees outside the Kornrumpf household. During daytime hours, the phone clattered constantly.

Telephones were an oddity for the family. Bi often laughed at Billie when she instinctively jumped up to reclaim the receiver.

Each evening when Earl pulled his car into the driveway, the window curtains would rumple at the sill, and four little eyes peered out at him. When Daddy America approached the house, the door would swing open as Bi ushered him in.

"'My daughter,'" he called her affectionately, "how are you?" . . . and Bi's face would beam with delight.

My and Tuan tugged at Earl's trousers, scrambling to be noticed. "*Ong noi, ong noi!*" they shouted as he stooped to collect a rash of juicy kisses.

Hanh, out of respect for his American father, rose to his feet, his absorption in English lessons taking second place to Earl. Hanh and Bi wanted desperately to adapt, and the first urgent step was communication. Thus, they spent four to six hours per day studying at the kitchen table.

"What did you do today, my son?" Earl boisterously asked Hanh as they shook hands each night.

Hanh replied, "Today . . . Hanh study English and I . . . what you say, Mommy?"

"You mowed the lawn!" Billie prompted from the kitchen.

Hanh shook his head. "I cannot say," he laughed. "I help my Da-dee," he said, as he steered an imaginary mower across the rug for Earl to see how he spent his time.

Sometimes Hanh carried firewood from the back yard to the fireplace in the living room. On other occasions he worked in the garden, pruned roses, or fixed a leak in the roof to please Daddy America.

Earl made a conscious effort to find jobs to keep him busy. It was important, he surmised, to preserve Hanh's dignity. Hanh reciprocated as he was able.

Every morning Hanh vacuumed while the children playfully dusted furniture. Enamored by Billie's modern kitchen, Bi scrubbed not only dishes, but the cupboards from top to bottom.

Bi feared electric appliances and refused to contend with the stove. Her poise was shaken by the red hot glow of its burners. When she tried to help

Bi blesses her hosts with a delicious Asian dish called *Mao-sai.*

Billie cook, her hands turned numb and clammy, so she insisted on doing dishes, instead.

—◁○▷—

One morning Billie took Bi by the arm, led her to the range, and said, "Bi, you cook today!"

"No, Mommy! Bi can not do!"

Billie was blunt. "Yes, Bi, you can. Mommy America will help you."

Bi stood feebly for a few moments, uncomfortable in her awkwardness.

Billie threw vegetables on the counter, and Bi pressed close. Soon she started chopping. Then, Billie stepped aside, sipped a cup of tea, and asked Bi a dozen questions about how she cooked in Vietnam.

Bi began to show Mommy America how she cooked in Vietnam. She stir-fried meat cubes with onion, and then added celery, tomato, and soy sauce. At the table, Bi dipped the concoction over cooked Ramen noodles. Billie and Earl enjoyed the delicious meal, complimenting her for her cooking finesse.

Afterwards, Billie asked Bi the name of the recipe.

"*Mao-sai,*" she said.

Billie thanked Bi profusely, as though she had made an immeasurable contribution, and indeed she had, for now she could share in the cooking.

Bi took pride in her cuisine and embellished the dining table, not only with *Mao-sai*, but also with fragrant roses beginning to blossom that spring. Confidence in her ability to produce a meal that her American parents enjoyed enhanced the young mother's pride. Her thin, drawn face filled out and blossomed.

5
Learning to Trust

Their Story Revealed

Four a.m. Earl twitched a pest from his forehead, then lapsed back to sleep. The nuisance bumbled across his face again. He flicked his hand to shoo it away. Abruptly, five determined appendages yanked vigorously at his nose.

"*Ong noi, ong noi,*" a rompish voice giggled. A slight brown body rolled over Earl and slid sidelong into Billie.

Earl raised himself on one elbow, his eyes blurred, and then fell back into his pillow and groaned.

"*Ong noi,*" the soft bundle chirped. He jabbered incessantly as Earl squinted his eyes in the early morning sunlight.

The brown face came into focus. Earl rubbed the sleep from his eyes. "Crawl in, Tuan," he managed wearily. In a moment's time, Tuan lunged his little body between Earl and Billie, intruding into their queen-sized bed. Only chipmunk cheeks and huge brown eyes peeked from the top of his nest.

◄o►

The equinox faded into Spring, and the family responded favorably to our members. They basked in Billie's love, and everyone gained weight except for Bi, who checked in at a meager 103 pounds.

Our congregation made a decision not to impose our religion on the family, yet nothing pleased us more than having Hanh and Bi among us on Sunday mornings. We were glad they came, as physical evidence of their presence built empathy among our parishioners. At the same time, I worried that they might not be accepted.

The following week, Adam and MiRan sank into the pew beside me. I glanced over my shoulder, anticipating the service, which would begin shortly. Sunlight flooded through stained glass windows creating a warm, orange glow. The people were chatty and cordial as the organ strained with voluminous music of the resurrection.

Anticipation pervaded the atmosphere on this beautiful Easter morning. Billie caught my eye across the aisle. Looked tired and drawn, but content, she wagged her finger in the opposite direction. I strained my neck to see.

There they sat. My nestled in her mother's lap gawking curiously at the strange surroundings. Tuan perched on Earl's knee, while Hanh sat in contemplative silence twitching his fingers nervously. I felt a warm glow start deep inside me and spread throughout my being. *Good,* I thought. *I'm glad they're here.*

After a set of hymns, one sung with gusto and one without, Herb walked down from the pulpit as he did each Sunday. There among the people, he shared our joys and sorrows.

Herb was just as thrilled as I to see the family there. His face glowed with the satisfaction of mission begun as he introduced the foursome.

Suddenly, and without warning, Hanh politely rose to his feet. He bowed slightly, and then boldly spoke to the entire congregation—in English. "Tank you veddy much," he said.

Verbal smiles darted around the sanctuary, and everyone 'ah-h-hed' at his achievement. Many appeared amazed that he possessed the courage to stand among a multitude of strangers. For all Hanh lacked in the language, his spirit overcompensated.

After the morning prayer, our daughter, MiRan, started bouncing next to me in the pew. She cupped her palms and whispered, "What's Daddy doing?"

I looked closely. Herb had retreated to the pulpit to preach the morning sermon, and then, just as MiRan intimated, he reached beneath the lectern and withdrew a lug wrench and a crowbar.

Oh, no! I thought, *Why is he preaching* that *sermon?*

To my horror, he wrenched them against his forehead to simulate a masochistic whipping.

Oh, Herb, why today? I ached silently as he launched into a theological exposition of how we sometimes browbeat ourselves and become our own worst enemies. But it was too late now. What did the family think? That Herb was contriving new methods of torture?

When he finally concluded with "God forgives us in spite of our shortcomings," I thought, *Oh, I hope so, Herb. I hope so.*

The service finished, I elbowed my way through the crowd to greet the family. When I finally located them, they were surrounded by church people. Mary was hugging Bi.

"We're so happy you came to Bryan," she said as she pecked Bi on the cheek and stood with her in support.

Our parishioners crowded around the family, one by one, welcoming them:

"We're happy you came today."

"You have such beautiful children."

Initial appraisal meshed into acceptance. These brown and yellow foreigners didn't look like enemies, after all. They were people, too.

The question loitered in the back of my mind: If the Vietnamese are human beings with souls, why were we over there killing them?

Some hugged. Others wrapped their arms around the children. The men subjected Hanh to measured looks, and then pumped his hand until he laughed, not knowing how to respond to them. The family felt awkward, but welcomed the church's embrace that Sunday morning.

◄○►

"One!" Earl scuttled the ball to Tuan.

"Du!" Tuan retorted.

"T'ree!" My continued. She felt better now and even ate the strange foods set before her.

"Foah!" Tuan chortled.

Earl missed 'five' deliberately. The children wrestled him playfully to the floor. Earl heard Tuan cackling, "*Ong noi, Ong noi!*"

Earl stopped short. "There it is again, Billie. That's what they keep saying." He turned to Hanh and Bi and, in encrypted English asked, "What Tuan say?"

"*Ong noi,*" the toddler piped again.

A smile softened Hanh's face. He looked at Daddy America and said, "Tuan say 'Grandpa' in Vietnamese."

Earl caught the lad and hugged him hard. My mistook the encounter for a 'love-in' and tumbled them both to the floor.

◄○►

Spring weather beckoned Bi outside to play with the children. The evening before, she and Hanh had strolled with them in the mossy woods near their bungalow, crinkling leaves from the previous fall.

Green patches of color sprouted on the maples. Closer examination revealed miniature replicas of leaves in development, some buds so fragile that their silhouettes seemed to protrude from the womb of the tree, still red with the blood of recent birth.

While blackberry bushes swayed in their verdue, caressing their branches were hundreds of white blossoms bursting into bloom. Beneath, in the shadows shoots were laden with buds, new promise of fruit—no famine for tomorrow.

The chilly spring air chased them inside, but not before Bi discovered a wild rose partially buried, but ever so carefully nourished by a bed of rotting leaves. She shouldered her way toward an object that resolved itself in the shape of a thorny bush. Pushing the stems aside, the rose's blossoms sprung out and delighted her. Leaning over, her nimble fingers plucked a sprig of leafy grandeur . . . "for Mommy Ame'dica," she told the children.

Like a child enamored with dandelions, Bi proudly presented the rose to Billie. The surrogate mother squeezed Bi's shoulders and basked in the warmth she felt for her new daughter.

—◦—

That Saturday the Kornrumpfs were planning on dinner out to cel-ebrate their wedding anniversary. The youthful grandmother, whose white curls betrayed the glint in her eyes, pinned the bud to her lapel before she and Earl left that evening.

"Maybe we shouldn't leave them alone," Billie worried aloud as they closed the door behind them.

Earl persisted. "But we need time for ourselves, too, honey."

The couple had sacrificed their privacy for a cause that they believed in, but Earl ached for private time for the two of them together.

Sensing their discomfort, Hanh insisted they go. Earl was relieved.

Billie had just fastened the last gold button on her navy blazer when a knock came at the door.

Jim, their neighbor, sported a bucket of smelt and an oversized grin. "We thought you could use these, since you have a houseful," he said. Then he handed the fish to Billie.

"Oh, Jim," she blurted. "We don't have time to clean them!"

Bi stepped spritely to her side. "Bi do, Mommy. Hanh, Bi do. Mommy 'n' Daddy go away tonight."

Billie's mouth gaped open, startled. Then she thought, *Why not? They have a need to give back, too.*

Earl donned his suede hat as the couple wielded knives over the buck-et, dishpans in their laps. Hanh shot a series of discordant phrases to Bi.

Earl sensed Hanh's discomfort.

Billie glanced at Earl, then turned to Hanh and asked, "Does Hanh like to clean fish?"

Hanh looked at Billie stiffly, held fast by ancient instinct. "In Vietnam," he swooped his arm toward the catch, " . . . women's work!"

Bi raised her head from the bucket where she was scraping entrails. Her grin dissolved the tension. "Hanh in Ame'dica now!"

Earl glanced at Billie, then took a deep gulp of air and smiled wryly as they stepped over the threshold and closed the door behind them.

An unbridled surge of laughter soared toward the treetops.

—◦—

"Oh, Mommy, Mommy," Bi sobbed. Her family had risked pirates and wild seas to come to America, hoping to find some peace, but the cruel twist of history and memories continually resurfaced.

More than once Billie comforted the young mother by rocking Bi in her arms as though she were a starling with a badly broken wing.

One afternoon, while musing over a photo album, Bi's eyes misted over. "Bi, Hanh, cry, cry," she said. Fluttering her fingers over her lashes, her slight frame quivered as she wept. Billie sighed hopelessly, and then, she hugged her Vietnamese daughter. She wanted so desperately to help her.

Hanh intercepted and the conversation turned to Uncle, who made possible his family's flight to freedom.

"Where does Uncle live now, Hanh?" Earl inquired.

Their English lessons were paying off, as Hanh was becoming more fluent.

"Uncle in Ame'dica, Daddy."

Earl looked stunned. "In America?" he reiterated. "You mean you have relatives here?"

Hanh detailed his story, as best as he could.

"Nor' Vietnam come Hanh's house. Hanh no like."

Already he was at a loss for words. He plucked The Book from the shelf, which lay at arms' length these days, and leafed hurriedly through the R's.

"Daddy, look! Look here," he insisted.

Rearranging his lanky body on the lounge, Earl peered through the bottom of his bifocals. "Resist?" he asked.

"Yeah," Hanh answered. "Hanh no like Nor' Vietnam. Nor' Vietnam steal Uncle farm. Hanh cannot work. Hanh . . . what you say?"

"Resisted," Earl finished.

Hanh continued. "Nor' Vietnam boom, boom Hanh's house." His arms stretched high, as if shooting an imaginary weapon.

"I send Bi, wit' my children to Uncle. Nor' Vietnam take Hanh . . . " he searched The Book for the precise word, "to 'ch . . . '?"

Earl looked over his shoulder to see where he was pointing. "To 'jail'?" Earl asked.

"Yes, Daddy. To 'chail.'"

Bi felt the heat tingling in her cheeks. "My, Tuan, Uncle 'n' me," she pointed to herself, "don' know where my husban', ef'ry day, ef'ry day. Don' know."

Hanh continued their gruesome saga, plucking words from the top of his cranium . . . "Hanh, on chair." He tilted a kitchen ladderback, placing his hand on the seat. "Un'erstand, Daddy?"

Hanh met Earl's gaze and stared at him intently, waiting for an answer. Earl's eyes fixed on Hanh. "Go on."

Hanh rose to his feet. An intense fire burned in his eyes as he placed himself in the chair. His gaze darted from Earl to Billie, then back again. He had survived and had to talk, for only in the re-telling could the tragedy be averted again.

He slid into a half-reclining position, his arms twined around the rungs, to simulate his torture. Dropping his head backwards, the blood beat coarsely in his throat. Strained words rasped hoarsely through his lips: "Nor' Vietnam beat, beat Hanh, ef'ry day, ef'ry day!"

Bi interrupted the conversation. "Nor' Vietnam hurt my husban'." She boxed her fists and pointed to her feet, her face flushed red.

"They kicked him?" Billie asked. She felt the indignation boiling up in her system.

Hanh answered bitterly. "Heah!" He pointed to his stomach. "Ev'ry day Nor' Vietnam kick." He tightened his fists in anger at his oppressors.

Bi shook her head in horror, mouth agape, reliving the scene with her husband. My and Tuan sat deafeningly still, rolling their eyes from mother to father. They dared not move when their parents spoke of this.

Earl abruptly rose to his feet and pounded his iron-clad fist against the wall. "How can people be so calloused toward other human beings?" he spat into the air.

Hanh did not flinch at Earl's outrage.

"Nor' Vietnam look, look for Hanh's Uncle. Nor' Vietnam cannot find. Uncle mus' hide Malaysia."

Stunned at his pronouncement, Billie proceeded cautiously. "Is Uncle still in Malaysia? Where does Uncle live now, Hanh?"

The question defused Hanh's anger, and his stockinged feet slipped deftly back to their bedroom. He reappeared with the duffle bag, rummaged a bit, and produced a crumpled paper.

There it was, his name, in San Diego, California, followed by a phone number.

Uncle was sponsored by Vietnamese friends living in San Diego. He managed to arrive in the states before Hanh. Soon after Uncle left Pulau Bidong, Hanh followed to Ohio two thousand miles away.

That night Earl and Billie allowed the family a ten-minute call to San Diego. Hanh did not seem happy to make the connection. He spoke long and intensely with Uncle.

When they signed off, he clicked the cold wrist of the receiver, dejected.

Earl glared at him. "What did Uncle say?"

Sadly and slowly, Hanh lifted his eyes to Daddy America. "He want my family come Calnifornya."

6

I Baptize You

A Christian Ritual, Revisited

There comes a premonition, a sensing, a knowing,
a picture in our minds not of our own,
but one that is painted for us.

As a church, we fully realized that the Nguyens might eventually resettle with Uncle. We did not feel that we could, or should, hold onto them forever. It only seemed fair that My and Tuan could grow to adulthood with a sense of family, since that possibility was now a reality.

Sponsorship, we reasoned, was similar to rearing a child from infancy to adolescence. Like parents weaning teenagers, we could only hope that once they left us, their fledgling spirits would know what they needed to know to survive.

I sauntered aimlessly down the streets of Bryan, mechanically crossing one chore after another off my list. The squeals of children playing wafted up from the courthouse square across the street.

The courthouse edifice was a magnificent structure, to be sure, an imposing mansion of nineteenth century vintage. It seemed a bit out of character for our sleepy, midwestern town. Yet its Gothic spires, rising high into the sky, made a statement as its four-faced clock tower ticked away the lives of those who walked beneath it.

The watermelon scent of freshly mowed grass beckoned MiRan toward the swings. Her little round face perked up at me, eyes squinting in the sun. "Mommy, may I?" she chortled.

I nodded in the affirmative.

She slipped her tiny hand into my larger one, and we traipsed across the street to play. Shading my eyes from the midday sun, I watched her scamper from the see-saw to the climber. She had been so patient with my chores that morning that I simply had to reward her.

Nestling into a park bench, I noted the low buildings across the street. They appeared to be swabbed with shoe polish and set in the sun to dry. Robins glided in narrow paths to their nests in the courthouse pinnacles, feeding their squawking young. The morning sun peaked and angled into afternoon as sparrows tried out abandoned nests for size.

An old pickup rattled by and brought me back to reality. There was Mi-Ran, in front of me, proudly displaying a bouquet of dandelions. I pecked her on the forehead and accepted her gift as she scampered back to the swings.

I felt comfortable with my thoughts. As quickly as we learned that Hanh and Bi had relatives in the states, we discovered that Uncle disowned him for disobeying his command to "come immediately to Calnifornya," something unheard of in Asian decorum.

Hanh refused, he said, because he cared for these people who so openly expressed love for his family. For the first time in his beleaguered life, Hanh said he experienced more than peace of mind. He had discovered 'happiness.'

We felt badly about the disagreement, but there was nothing we could do. The transaction was strictly between Hanh and Uncle. "In the meantime," I ventured smugly, "we are their surrogate family."

Little My and our daughter, MiRan, became the best of friends. Both were four years old and gloated in it. Tuan idolized Adam and often wrestled him to the floor as a gesture of affection in the basement after church.

◄◦►

And then, Herb did it. In keeping with Brethren tradition, he led a man into the baptistry and completed a trine immersion. We later learned that Hanh thought Herb was giving the fellow a bath[5].

Sunlight bathed through the windows in a soft yellow wash. This was a moving moment for our church. The lone figure silhouetted against the baptistry was a man who, for years, refused to be baptized, feeling it unnecessary. Now at age forty-five, he finally made the decision.

I looked for his family and saw Phyllis, his wife, weeping. Fern and Bob, his in-laws, managed to check their emotions.

As I turned toward the chancel again, I glanced at Billie. She had a far-away look in her eyes, the scene carrying her across time and space.

"I baptize you in the name of the Father . . . and of the Son . . . and of the Holy Spirit." Beyond the scope of her limited understanding, Billie was haunted by the memory of those words. The prisms in her eyes saw a dozen Herbs and a dozen others being baptized, and she was one of them. How well she recalled that morning when she, Willena Kornrumpf, stepped into the baptismal pool. She sat on the step because her leg was inflamed with phlebitis, and the pain was too great for her to kneel.

"Mrs. Kornrumpf," the doctor had told her, "we've done all we can do. The blockage in your right leg is severe, and I regret to tell you . . ."

The bespeckled man in white droned on.

Billie startled from her euphoria, her face chilled and drawn. He didn't say "amputation," did he? Had she heard him correctly?

But she had.

Billie shuddered and broke into tears, and Earl wept with her. This was not the first time, for she had wakened many times, only to find him sitting by her hospital bed, painfully aware of his powerlessness. During the years of her illness, a clot had entered Billie's right lung forcing surgeons to excise a portion of it in emergency surgery.

The conflagration could not be extinguished, and months later, phlebitis struck again, nearly taking her life. Another clot blocked the artery in her right leg so completely that her stomach swelled to the size of a pregnant woman as blood accumulated in her abdominal cavity.

This time, the clots persisted, and immediate surgery was necessary. She lay in the hospital for months, heavily drugged to sedate the pain.

Earl stayed faithfully by her side. More often than not, she awakened to find him holding her hand, his eyes moist with tears. There was no one he loved more than Billie, and she was slowly slipping away from him.

And then, one overcast morning in November, Herb walked into her hospital room. He spoke with her and counseled her. A long list of hurts had followed throughout her life. She had no church, no pastor, no friend to share her burden, except for Earl. She had borrowed on his strength as long as she could, and now she was ready to die.

Love is listening to another, and so Herb listened. As Billie emptied her bitter soul, she began to weep. Herb grasped her hand and told her to cry . . . cry hard and loud and long . . . to get the ugliness out of her system.

She did. And then they prayed.

When Earl arrived the next morning, Billie's surgeon had made an emergency appointment for her at Mayo Clinic with the prospect of amputation.

---

[5] The Church of the Brethren originated in Germany in 1708 with a sect called the Dunkers. Dunkers immersed, or 'dunked' new converts in running water for baptism. Many Brethren churches were constructed near rivers for this reason. Thus, the 'Lick Creek Church of the Brethren.'

"Billie, why won't you listen?" Earl begged her. "If the doctor says you must go, you must go!"

"Earl," she said, "there are two things I must do before we leave for Mayo. Do you promise we can do them?" Her eyes implored her husband of thirty-five years to answer in the affirmative.

Earl cradled her hands in both of his. "I'll do anything for you, honey."

"I want to fly to Virginia to see Sandy and . . . ," she paused.

". . . and what, Billie?"

"I want to be baptized."

Earl peered deeply into his wife's eyes. "All right," he said, and kissed her. "Let's do it."

—◄o►—

A few days before leaving for Mayo, Billie stood before the congregation and told them of her intentions. The expectant look on their waiting faces radiated empathy from our members.

She propped her body against the pew, with her distressed leg against it. She could not bear pressure on her foot, even for a minute. She felt absurdly small, engulfed by the crowd that morning as she addressed them.

"Earl and I have trials to face in the next few weeks," she said. "We can't do it alone. This morning I'm going to be baptized . . . because I need the power of God with me as I face a difficult decision."

Her lips quivered, and I felt a surge of tenderness for her vulnerability.

Then she stepped forward, ready.

Herb grasped her hands and steadied her as she lowered her body into the baptistry. She sat on the step because she could not flex her leg to kneel.

As water was poured over her head and trickled down her spine, the familiar words echoed their refrain down through the centuries . . ., "I baptize you in the name of the Father . . . and of the Son . . . and of the Holy Spirit."[6]

An unaccustomed heat rose steadily through Billie's body as a great and heavy burden lifted from her shoulders. She breathed deeply and relaxed for the first time in many months.

—◄o►—

The Kornrumpfs spent a quiet Christmas at home. The following day they left for Mayo. That morning Herb extracted a promise from Earl that he would call as soon as the specialists had completed her surgery.

---

6 Matthew 28: 19

One day lapsed, and then two. A third day passed without a report. Herb called Earl's motel, but still, no answer.

I'm not surprised, he thought. *Earl isn't near a phone, and he's preoccupied with Billie. She needs him now more than ever.*

Five days later, Billie called.

"Herb, I'm home!" she shouted into the phone.

Ecstatically, she recounted the events of the past few days. Every medical report, every exam, every X-ray and blood test that proved problematic in Bryan, when repeated at Mayo, came out clear.

Bewildered, the surgeon scheduled a private consultation. There was no need for amputation, he said. She still had phlebitis, but a mild case. If vigilant, she could lead a normal life.

That night in the hotel, Billie and Earl sat on the edge of their bed. The weight of the past few days flooded Billie's soul, and she began to weep. Earl's tired eyes stared at her for a moment, and then, the pent-up emotions of seven years of pain burst in a flood, unwinding like the tension in a spring. Tears mixed with joy as he gathered Billie in his arms.

"Earl," Billie choked. "This is the happiest day of my life. I'm well, honey. I'm whole."

The old tough soldier of bygone years held her tightly and wept in relief. She could support him now, for she was the one with strength.

Billie nuzzled her chin on Earl's shoulder. "Honey, you know Who did this, don't you?"

Earl opened his mouth to answer her, but the words wouldn't come.

And then, the strain of the last year released itself in one agonizingly beautiful moment. Looking from a distance, an Omniscient Observer could see a man and wife, clinging to each other with a love like they never knew before, sliding to the floor to pray. The bitterness and hurt of past years dissolved in the words reverberating from their hearts. . .

"I baptize you . . . in the name of the Father, and of the Son, and of the Holy Spirit."

7
Circles of Intimacy

Personal Needs

Hon, a vibrant young woman in her mid-twenties, trotted briskly to the door. "Ha-llo," she sang in her heavily accented English. "Come my house!"

She waved her arm in a dramatic gesture toward the small but modern apartment. Her pleasant demeanor quickly put Billie and me at ease.

Hon introduced her husband, Ming, a slight man with thick black hair and confident gait. Ming worked evenings for a local manufacturer.

Their two preschoolers eyed us apprehensively when we invaded their territory. Vi, the oldest, timidly backed into her father's arms while John Paul, their youngest, dragged My and Tuan back to his room to play. MiRan hovered next to me and watched them disappear down the hallway.

Like Bi and Hanh, Hon and Ming fled Vietnam in 1975 during the mass exodus out of the country. They journeyed to America via a huge ocean liner and quickly befriended the captain. "I tease him," said Hon, "and tell him if he don' get me to Ame'dica before my baby born, I will name baby for him."

The captain took pride posing as their symbol of freedom and lingered at sea long enough to witness the birth of a baby boy. The couple named him 'John Paul', as promised.

Ming pulled up a lounge chair for Hanh, then tilted his head forward. 'Si' down,' he said politely.

Hanh dropped into the recliner while Bi and Hon claimed the sofa. The couples talked expansively with each other in their mother tongue, leaving Billie and me on the sidelines.

I felt vaguely embarrassed sitting there, rather like an appendage, but Billie looked smug and relaxed. She darted a quick glance in my direction that said, "Let them talk their hearts out."

A few days later, Hon and her husband, Ming, drove with us to the Social Security office. It didn't take long for the confusing forms to thrust us into a quagmire.

The attendant on duty glared at us over wire-rimmed glasses. "The form is incomplete, madam. The computer has rejected it."

Her pursed lips told me that her statement was final.

Billie's spirits plummeted as we wandered back to our seats. "Bi needs a birthday," she said.

Hon offered her wisdom. "Bi say she born 1952. Her parents live far from city. When they register her birth, Bi's mother remember year, but not the day. She have no birthday, Billie." Her eyes expressed concern for Bi's dilemma.

Hanh rattled off a string of Vietnamese to Ming, who laughed perceptively.

"Hanh have similar problem," Hon stated. "His father register him when he two years old. Father have correct birthday, but wrong year. Hanh is one year older."

"So . . . how do we deal with this?" I asked.

"Easy," Hon said. "We write his legal age . . . the one on passport."

I looked at her, confused. "That'll work for Hanh, but it won't for Bi." Bi's passport was blank on the month and day.

Bi grinned a wily smile, as her eyes darted toward Billie.

"Mommy birthday?" she asked.

Billie looked surprised.

"January 12th," she said, "but what does my birthday have to do with this?" Her face softened at Bi's expression.

Bi tapped the blank space on the form. "Mommy birthday . . . January 12. Bi birthday . . . January 12!"

Billie felt an unaccustomed lump in her throat as warmth crept through her neck and flushed her beige complexion.

"You're my daughter, Bi," she gasped, as if to cover up a start.

◄○►

"No," Billie shook her head. "Daddy and Mommy not sponsor you. Church people sponsor you."

What was this strange phenomenon . . . 'church people'?

"Herb, Jeanne, they are 'church people'. And people who bring you food to eat." Earl pumped his arm in fork-to-plate motions. "They are church people, too." Bi's brow furrowed, working intently for understanding.

"Church people" welcome the Nguyen family into our fold. Adults, left to right: Mabel, Hanh, Bi, Wilma, and Nguyen children: My and Tuan

At first, they lumped everyone in our congregation into one indivisible whole, but later, as we mingled with them, our members took on names and personalities in their own right.

Florence and Wilma, their English teachers, began their long, tedious journey across the world of language. They painstakingly coached Bi in the grocery store and helped her compare prices. She quickly learned the word, "cheap!"

Occasionally, Billie brought Bi to our sewing circle. Before we secured a job for Hanh, sometimes he came with her to watch the children.

One Thursday morning, Bi positioned herself in the middle of the quilting ladies. After watching them for a while, she threaded a needle and joined them.

The ladies fell silent. Feeling awkward at Bi's presence, Mattie's eyes darted over to Fern, who ribbed Delphie with her elbow.

"What's the matter?" Delphie asked.

"Look who's sitting there," Fern retorted, not as sensitive as she should have been.

"Oh, she'll catch on," Delphie answered.

Fern's eyes darted across the comforter toward Joyce. "How can we possibly communicate with her?" she asked. "Bi doesn't understand a word we're saying!"

Delphie smiled awkwardly, and then, gave it a whirl.

"What's your name?" she asked.

Bi looked blankly at the coiffured lady, not knowing how to respond.

Delphie shrugged her shoulders. Then, hunching over the quilt, her needle perched vertically, she confessed to her cohorts, "I don't know what else to ask her!"

"We don't, either," retorted Fern, "but you said 'talk', so YOU talk!"

A sweetly dispositioned woman, Delphie often drew others into her circle, but this was challenging. How could they have a conversation with Bi when she didn't understand English?

Several eternal minutes lapsed. Finally, the teacher in me came to the rescue.

I rose from my chair and crossed the room. "Ladies," I said, "Just talk with her like you do with each other. Keep it simple, and Bi will learn by listening."

Dorothy asked, "But what should we talk about?"

"Anything. You know all that friendly gossip you ladies do all the time? Go at it!"

Hearing this coming from the preacher's wife, they glared at me and snickered.

—◦—

At first, Phyllis spoke gingerly, enunciating words like a nervous puppet. Then, Joyce chimed in from across the motley patchwork. Soon they jabbered at their usual rapid pace, taking time, here and there, to teach Bi some sewing vocabulary.

"'Scissors, yarn, needle,' Dorothy said, pointing to the items in her sewing basket. 'Can you say it, Bi? 'Scissors, yarn, needle.'

Bi shook her dark waves. She didn't understand . . . not even the simplest words in English.

Fern peered at Joyce with raised eyebrows. Then, holding her needle upright, she said, "Bi, watch me. See needle? Put needle here!"

Fern poked the steely splinter through the quilt. "Then catch the lining, like this."

"We . . . must . . . talk . . . slowly . . . right?"

In spite of our fumbled attempts, including Bi in our activities seemed an important thing to do. Until her English took hold, we did our best to communicate with pantomime and choppy language.

—◁o▷—

At noon we took a break from quilting and clustered a dozen chairs at the table. Bi joined us with the children, and Hanh dropped by for lunch.

After the meal, My gyrated a little red wagon, over-laden with toys, across the floor faster than her wiry little body could waddle. Joyce laced a shoe string into a punch-out card for Tuan, and he became her buddy.

Left to right: Tuan and My loved learning English with picture books.

Mattie resumed her communication attempts with the family. "My daughter," she modulated, "will travel to Korea next week."

At a loss for words, Hanh chuckled benignly and, then, he looked toward me for a bail-out.

My brain scoured for a way to explain Mattie's comment. Suddenly, I knew.

"My is Bi and Hanh's daughter," I enunciated. "Mattie's daughter . . ."

I gestured toward her. "Mattie's daughter will go to Korea—Korea, 'same-same' country as MiRan."

The couple connected Korea and Mattie's daughter and made some sense of it.

—<o>—

Morning showers gave way to sunshine, and we made our way outside. I noticed Hanh's reflection on the rain-washed car and asked what he was thinking.

Before he pulled the door shut, he turned to me and said, "Ef'rybody luf' us."

Hanh told us what we needed to know.

His family felt our embrace, and that was what we had hoped for.

—<o>—

Back home that night, Hanh asked Billie again, "Mommy, why church people so good to us?"

Billie repeated her mantra, just as she had many times before:

"Because our God tells us to love you, Hanh. Because our God tells us to love you."

—<o>—

Spring arrived, and Earl and Hanh broke ground to begin planting. One afternoon Billie wandered outside, only to find Earl weeding the garden, dusty from the waist down.

"My dear," she laughed, as she slipped her arm around his shoulder, "Already the buds are beginning to blossom."

Earl looked inquisitively at Billie. What did she mean? He lifted his eyes and caught their glimmer.

Then she leaned over and kissed him.

8
Little One Lost

"They Left a 'What' Still There?"

We stepped into the doctor's office on a rainy Wednesday. The afternoon sprinkling pattered the windows outside as we shook our dripping umbrellas in the atrium.

The receptionist's dark hair, caught up at the back of her neck, formed a bun. Ushering us into the waiting room, she gave us the perfunctory forms and asked us to take seats.

I quickly surveyed the long list of questions.

To spare Bi the anxiety of the visit, Hon volunteered to come with us to serve as Bi's interpreter.

I breathed a heavy sigh . . . *Forms, forms, forms! Too many forms!* With Bi's limited language skills, how could we possibly answer all the information they needed?'

Hon spoke in a quiet voice as she translated the nurse's questions, looking to Bi for answers. I jotted notes on what transpired so we would have them for future reference.

"Where were her babies born?

"At home."

"Did she have prenatal care?

"What is pre- . . .?" Hon stumbled.

Hon bantered the question back and forth with the nurse, while I checked the dictionary for a simpler way to ask it. Nothing helpful surfaced.

The nurse went on. Did she have a doctor or midwife?"

"Baby born, midwife," Hon said.

"When was her last gynecological exam?"

"She don' know what that is," Hon added.

On and on the questions went. My pen struggled to keep pace with Hon's translation as she unraveled Bi's answers.

I stole a prolonged look at Hon, marveling at her efficiency. She was an attractive woman, short in height, with black, sleek hair cascading over her shoulders. It complimented the golden tone of her skin. My appreciation of her was heightened by her straight-forward manner of dealing with the interminable number of questions.

"How many pregnancies?" the nurse asked.

Bi's eyes reflected silence.

In my mind, I counted two, My and Tuan.

"Two", I wrote.

Hon leaned close to hear Bi's answer.

"Four," she answered.

Her answer caught me by surprise. "You mean two?" I corrected.

"No, four," she enunciated, this time more clearly.

Billie's mouth gaped open, waiting for an explanation. "Four?" She counted Bi's pregnancies visibly on her hand.

Hon's head shook soberly. Her tender eyes pleaded with us to listen.

"You don' un'erstand. One baby die when born, Vietnam," she said, looking to us for empathy, "and she haf' a baby still there."

Hon's words dropped like a gossamer thread in thin air. They flooded our heats with emotions we were not expecting.

Billie gasped, "But that's impossible."

"She do, Billie," Hon repeated. "She haf' a baby still there."

Yet Billie could not deny the truth Hon had spoken. Catching her breath, she stymied her emotions and spoke, in monotone.

"She has a baby still there?"

"Yeah," Hon drawled. Her delicate face showed pre-mature wrinkles. Four years of separation from her own family had taken their toll. They were part of war's collateral.

"She haf' a baby daughter there, only seventeen month old."

Our eyes focused on Bi, her hands shaking in tremor. The slippery grip she had on life suddenly let loose and she broke down, weeping. We finally understood her.

Billie hurried to Bi's side and crackled in a whisper, "Bi, we didn't know. Why didn't you tell us, honey?"

Hon's sensitive eyes pleaded with Billie as Bi sobbed uncontrollably.

"She try to, Billie . . . several times." Hon shook her head, resigned.

Billie reached for Bi and wrapped her in her wings like a mother starling. In that moment Mommy America became a bastion of defense against the cold and lonely world.

"She try make you un'erstand, but didn't know how," Hon said.

I buried my head in the pile of forms, choking back hot tears. *Oh, the forms, so many miserable forms!* I wanted to lash out against the unjust powers that allowed these things to happen.

Oh, Bi and Hanh, I wailed to myself, *you've lived through hell on earth!*

Bi was quiet now. Gazing in a trance-like state into the shadows of the hallway, they mirrored her isolation.

"Isn't there something we can do, Jeanne?" Billie implored. "I mean, anything at all?"

My thirsty eyes looked ruefully at her, searching for an answer.

Swallowing the lump in my throat, I rasped, "I don't know. If we could somehow negotiate with Vietnam, then, maybe."

I scanned the farthest recess of my memory for a shred of hope. A year of legal experience with a judge in Pennsylvania had lent me a wealth of information that I often found expedient, but this was international, and that was a different matter.

"Hon," I asked, "You've been here four years. Have you communicated with your family back home?"

"Only last week," she said. "I get letter, my mother. She write it four year' ago. Tha's all."

A shiver ran down my spine. The immensity of the problem seemed overwhelming. As hard as we might try, I doubted anything could be done. *Yet, if this were my child,* I thought, *I would try and try again.*

I knew it would take a miracle for anything to happen, but the last glimmer of light in Bi's eyes would vanish altogether if we didn't, at least, make an effort.

That night I lay awake for hours tossing their circumstances in my mind.

◄○►

The next morning I was ready to begin my search, but first I checked in with Billie.

"Did you learn anything new?" I asked. Every shred of information took on new significance now.

"I did, Jeanne. Hanh's parents have the baby. Bi and Hanh fled when she was just six months old. They were afraid she'd cry and give them away in hiding. She was too little to make the journey."

"Have they corresponded?"

"Since they left, they tried sending letters to Vietnam, but no one has written back."

I hugged the phone closer. "They'll have to know we're trying to get her, Billie."

"Like, how?"

"We're ahead of ourselves," I surmised. "We don't even know if it's possible to get a letter through. Vietnam is Communist now."

As an afterthought, I asked, "Bi and Hanh want to make contact, don't they?"

"Of course, they do," she said.

The silence drew taunt between us. How could we possibly retrieve anything, let alone a baby, from a Communist country? It seemed we held an awesome, dangerous secret in our hands.

Billie posed. "I don't know how to do this any more than you do."

"Have they tried every avenue?" I asked. "If letters can't get through because of the hostilities between our countries, we'll have to outwit the system."

"What about Canada?" Billie asked. "My cousin and his wife live there. Do you think . . . ?"

"Sure! Let's try!"

"Good!" Billie replied. "I'll send Hanh and Bi's letters to my cousin and his wife and see if they can forward them from there."

This was a start, I thought. *If all works out, we would need to get word to Bi's parents so they would know what was happening. Otherwise, if the day arrived when Bi and Hanh called for their baby, they might be afraid to release her.*

The thought was very encouraging.

—<o>—

But where to begin? No matter the venue, we would have to navigate our own government's regulations. Pacing back and forth in the kitchen, I found a number and dialed it.

"Immigration, New York City," a tiny voice chanted on the other end of the line. "Please stand by."

A few minutes later, the agent returned. After hearing our request, she asked brashly, "But why are you calling *us*? What does our office have to do with this matter?"

I was stunned at her rudeness. Didn't she have any leads, any suggestions at all?

She didn't.

I started at the phone blankly, and then hung up. *Strange,* I thought, *how one cares nothing about a situation unless it intimately concerns her. That agent has no schema for suffering.*

For an hour I sat there wondering who else we might contact . . . *What next?*

―◄○►―

Adam banged on the front door.

Three o'clock already? I thought. Running to the screen door, I ushered him in.

He waded into the living room loaded down with his bookbag, lunch box, and a grocery sack stacked to the brim.

MiRan scampered to her brother's rescue.

"What da ya' haf' there?" she asked, all in a single breath.

"School things," he puffed. "Miz Dierks said we hafta clean our desks an' get organized before school's over." He plopped the grocery sack on the sofa.

MiRan dove into the pile.

"Hey!" he reprimanded her, "Get outa there!"

"Can't you two get along for a single minute?" I yelled from the kitchen.

"Hey, Mom! Lookie here!"

Adam pulled out a picture he drew for art—the side view of an ant colony, above and underground, with tunnels leading to the queen, her nursery, and graveyard. Black straggly ants polluted the motley scene.

That's how I feel, I thought, *like an ant groping for an exit to the light.*

―◄○►―

"Hey, Mom, wanna play a game of chess?"

Encouraged the night before when he won two out of three to his Daddy, Adam was eager to try his skills again.

"All right," I answered, halfheartedly.

We played the first round. The little fellow sported a definite offensive and licked me soundly.

"So Dad's been teaching you strategy?" I quipped.

Adam ignored my question, and set up another round.

I sighed. *So this is what happens when you're forced to play a game without knowing the rules?*

Suddenly, I realized I was sitting there playing chess and perched by the phone expecting it to ring, yet I hadn't initiated a single call that could generate any promising possibilities.

I glared at the handset. Whom to call next? There surely had to be someone who could advise us. Unfortunately, I had an aversion for talking with strangers, especially those who wielded power. I could do it and often did, particularly when working for a judge a few years earlier, but I never relished those tasks.

I swallowed hard and lifted the receiver before I lost my courage.

Perhaps the Methodists up the road could advise us. They had sponsored a Laotian family and might have some suggestions.

Slowly, I dialed their number.

Their secretary was helpful. She had a son in Washington, DC who gave her a name and the phone number of the Refugee Task Force. "They're efficient and will answer your questions without hesitation," she told me.

—◁o▷—

Minutes later I dialed again. "May I speak with Mr. Sponga?"

A strong accent greeted me on the other end of the line. "Mr. Sponga ees not here at dis time. May he return your call, ma'dam?"

"Yes, please. My number is . . ."

—◁o▷—

An hour later the phone rang.

Mr. Sponga was sensitive and understanding, with accumulated insights into the refugees' situations. Undoubtedly, he heard my story many times before. He knew the heartbreak and utter frustration that refugees felt when loved ones were displaced.

"You will have to proceed through the State Department," he said, "but your family must apply for a visa for the child here in the U.S. before anything can happen abroad."

My pen whisked across the paper, jotting information as fast as he could generate it. "What forms do we need?" I asked.

"Forms I-130 and I-134," he answered. "If the child's visa is approved here in the U.S., it will be sent to the American Embassy in Thailand. They, in turn, will transfer the visa to the French Embassy in Bangkok. France still maintains diplomatic relations with Vietnam. That's complicated, I know, but . . ."

Struggling to transcribe as fast as he talked, I asked, "Speak more slowly, please, Mr. Sponga? I'm trying to jot all this down."

He hesitated. "Do you have it now?"

"Yes . . . go on."

"In Vietnam the French Embassy will send a letter to the child's grand-parents. You have their address, I presume?"

"We'll get it," I assured him.

"Good," he said. "Then, the grandparents must travel to the embassy and present the forms for your baby to receive asylum. If, and I repeat, 'IF' their government releases her, she will travel to Bangkok and from there, to the United States."

My mind whirled with questions that he answered most efficiently.

"Fine," he said. "I'll call the State Department immediately and have them send you the document, for Family Reunification, that is. The answers to your questions will be there."

I was extremely grateful for Mr. Sponga's kindness. In a matter of moments, my mood swung wildly from the darkest pessimism to an aria of elation.

At home I dialed Billie promptly with the hopeful news.

"Great!" she responded, excited as much as I was, but in the course of our conversation a worried tone filtered her voice. "There's been a new development, Jeanne. I don't know what to make of it."

I was curious about what had transpired.

"Hanh tells me now that he doesn't even know if his parents are still alive."

She continued, "He's afraid the North lashed out against them because he absconded. They could have, you know."

I sighed, " . . . especially if they thought his family aided and abetted him. What now?"

"Let's proceed as though they're alive unless there's reason to believe otherwise."

◄○►

Back at the office, Herb paced the floor, dictating the letter while I typed:

"To the Honorable Delbert Latta, U.S. Congress:

We, the members of the Church of the Brethren in Bryan, Ohio, request your assistance in a matter of grave concern to us . . . "

Herb cupped his chin in his hands, organizing his thoughts as I transcribed. He continued. "We request that the two-year waiting period for the Nguyen infant be waived . . . so that she may avoid extensive psychological problems in adjustment at a later date."

◄○►

Three weeks later, Congressman Latta responded. The Family Reunification form was detailed, but helpful. Unfortunately, the two-year waiting period could not be waived, a fact that proved disheartening.

But if we waited too long, Bi and Hanh would be strangers when their daughter arrived. We had to act quickly.

9
Settling In

A Cozy Apartment Awaits Them, but They Don't Like It One Bit.

Mommy, why we mus' go?" Bi's frightened voice sobbed through the silence. "We do somet'ing bad, Mommy?"

On the verge of tears all day, the flood gates finally opened and Bi's emotions flowed freely. The church's decision to move them into their own apartment made no sense whatsoever. Bi thought her family was being punished because they did something wrong.

Billie's heart sunk. "Bi," she tried to explain, "you and Hanh did not do anything wrong."

Frustrated at her inability to unravel their cross-cultural conundrum, Billie pushed her centerpiece across the table and prematurely called it finished. Exasperation at her inability to explain the move to the little Asian couple resulted in her weeping with them.

Again, she tried to explain how parents and their grown children live independently of each other in the United States.

"Mommy, we like lif' here," the young mother whimpered. "In Vietnam Hanh 'n' Bi lif' wit' Mommy 'n' Daddy, same-same."

Billie searched futilely for a way to explain, and then, she resigned the task to Hanh. "Hanh, you tell Bi why you can't live with Mommy and Daddy in America."

At a loss for words, he flustered, "I don' know. I cannot say." He hung his head in shame, his mind a battleground of conflicting values. He didn't understand, either.

In Vietnam, we eventually learned, extended families live together collectively and not in individual homes. The very thought of a family living alone terrified them. Indeed, it challenged their cultural identity. If an adult child lacked piety for an elder, he was shunned, not only by the next of kin, but by the entire community.

Billie sat quietly, thinking.

"Hanh," she explained, "In America Mommy and Daddy live in one house. Son number one gets married. He moves with his family to another house. Son number two gets married. He moves with his family to his house. Church people say you and Bi must have your house, too."

Bi raised her head, her countenance pale. Hanh's eyes glazed over, trying to look brave. Forcing a slight smile, he tried to mollify Mommy America.

Billie sensed a tenuous breakthrough, then, added weakly, "Hanh, your family can come to my house for dinner every Thursday."

Her generous offer proved little consolation for the distraught couple who felt banished from their sanctuary.

Hanh lowered his gaze and said, "Mommy," "I not happy we mus' go. My wife, she t'ink she un'erstand, but she not happy, too."

Like a wounded animal, he rose from his chair and with a long sigh, spoke to his surrogate mother.

Billie's observant eyes watched him articulate each syllable.

"In Vietnam," he said, "I marry Bi. She lif' my father house wit' me. She help my mother cook, clean, ef'ry day. My 'n' Tuan, born my father house."

Billie paused, then added, thoughtfully, "So, you think Daddy and I do not love you because you must live in your own house? Hanh, we love you very much, but in America married couples have their own homes.

"You see," she continued, "Daddy and Mommy are 'leaders' in this house. When Son Number One gets married, he and his wife are 'leaders' in their house. Son Number Two, same-same. Now, Hanh and Bi must have their own house, too."

Billie implored him to understand. "We still love your family, Hanh."

Hanh sulked in his seat, accepting her explanation with as much grace as he could muster. "Okay, Mommy. We do what you 'n' Daddy say."

◄o►

Asian wisdom dictated that Hanh and Bi live with his family to care for their elders. The insubordination of a child who relinquished that duty would dishonor the family. In Vietnam, if a child, regardless of age, lacks filial piety and respect, that child is ostracized by the community.[7]

Yet in America, this strange custom required that they abandon their surrogate family, the antithesis of everything honorable and upright in Vietnam.

---

7 See Vietnam Online: Family – "Relationships Among Family Members in Vietnam." http://www.vietnamonline.com/culture/family.html . July 6, 2015.

The Nguyen family in their apartment dining room

Deeply hurt and feeling rejected, Hanh must have thought to himself, *"Customs . . . empty headed customs!"*

And freedom, too, Hanh. In America, independence and making one's own decisions are the bedrock of freedom.

―◄o►―

That Thursday Sharon and I scrubbed cupboards and waxed the floors in their new apartment. Her contagious laughter rang through the flat as our church people unloaded boxes of kitchen utensils, a truck of donated furniture, and a used black and white TV.

The television was a matter of contention. Would the constant presence of English offset the less desirable programming?

"I hope it will," said Wilma who, as a former teacher, had personal stake in the question.

In the early afternoon, Fern and Bob arrived with buckets and a fresh supply of cleaning towels. Before they dove into their tasks, Fern plopped a voluminous bouquet on the dining room table. She proceeded to the kitchen, determined to fetch Bi and bring her in to see them.

Bi followed obediently as Fern guided her toward the table.

"Here's for your new apartment, Bi!" she almost shouted.

A few of Fern's acquaintances were on the verge of deafness so she instinctively raised the volume to help them understand her. Didn't it follow logically that turning up the decibels would do the same for the family? They couldn't understand her, either.

Fern was not alone. Others fell prone to the misconception. Had they thought for a moment about why they were shouting, they would have enjoyed a good and lusty laugh.

A few minutes later, I scuttled to the kitchen to catch a glimpse of Fern's bouquet. There they were in an old blue Mason jar. Between clusters of lilacs, four delicate rose buds reared their bobbing heads, almost unnoticed in the labyrinth.

While the bountiful lilacs added a touch of spring to their apartment, the roses, in their fragility, seemed something almost spiritual. Indeed, they were four new lives beginning to blossom.

Moments later, Billie slipped up behind me. Darting her eyes around to see if we were alone, she whispered, "Jeanne, do you know what happened the other night?"

I shook my head 'no'.

"They thought they were going to live with us . . . like parents and grown children do in Vietnam. After we told them about the apartment, Hanh laid his head on my lap and wept. They didn't want to leave.

"Last night they gave us a thank you gift."

She swallowed hard and choked. "I'm sorry. I'll tell you the rest later."

I left Billie alone with her emotions, and she returned to her task.

Herb and I were the last to go, leaving Bi and Hanh alone in their new apartment. Autonomy and independence from parents were new concepts for them. Indeed, they were downright frightening.

◄o►

That Friday, we made a trek to the telephone office. Back at their apartment, Hanh watched as Herb clicked the mechanism into the switchbox on the wall. While he dialed to check the connection, I recorded important phone numbers in the back of their directory.

The family's apartment was empty enough to permit tricycle riding by My and Tuan.

Hanh crossed his arms, perturbed. "Phone?" he mused. "Why phone?" He shook his head. "Hanh not speak so much English."

"Herb, Hanh wonders why he needs a phone," I said. "Tell him!"

Herb lifted the receiver, gears clicking in his head. He never had to explain a telephone before. Cradling the handset in his hands, he tried to reduce his explanation to the lowest common denominator.

"Hanh, if something is not right, and you and Bi need help, use this phone to call Herb and Jeanne, or Mommy and Daddy. If you say, 'Come!' we will come."

Hanh listened half-heartedly, but acquiesced completely when we told him he could call Chung if he had any questions.

◄○►

We meandered into the living room with its newly starched curtains. Two end tables, a couch, a rocker, lamps and throw rugs graced the room. Fern's bouquet overwhelmed the top of the dinette, lending a casual elegance to the otherwise alien atmosphere.

Off to the side in the dining area, four vintage chairs donated by one of our families had been refurbished with a bottle of scratch polish. MiRan's outgrown booster chair completed the cozy scene. Even the wall hangings from our dusty attics looked like they belonged.

Bi sank into the sofa, wiping her weary brow. The prosaic surroundings brought little comfort to her. Like Hanh, she, too, was afraid to live alone.

I gave a furtive glance in Herb's direction.

"Herb, we need to warn them about Sam," I said, cramming a can of Comet into a bucket.

Herb eyed me wearily. "I'd rather not right now." Then, shifting gears, he added, "You do it, but make it quick!"

"'Yeah, quick, Mom!" Adam echoed. "We're hungry!"

MiRan stretched her arms, feigning a yawn. "I'm tir-r-red," she crowed.

I knew full well that at home she would revive.

Looking askance at my husband, I tried again. "Herb, Hanh takes you more seriously. Please tell him about Sam!"

The reshuffling of responsibility exuded a groan from my husband.

Hanh had not liked the looks of Sam. I had seen him eye his neighbor earlier in the day with more than a hint of skepticism.

Sam's size, alone, was foreboding. His bulbous arms, facial grimaces, and slightly slurred speech heightened the family's apprehension. Added to their misgivings was Sam's hound which posed upright, its hind feet stiff, as if waiting to attack its prey. When strangers approached, however, its pupils rolled to the top of their sockets, curious enough to explore, but too apathetic to care. In such moments, its large brown eyes dispelled all notions of aggression.

"Herb, please!" I begged. "Sam is mentally unbalanced."

Herb glanced at me and sighed. "OK. Get The Book out, Jeanne."

We didn't want to frighten the family, but their neighbors warned us that Sam occasionally had outbursts that sometimes bordered on 'harrowing'. Their wisdom insinuated that we warn Hanh and Bi so they could be watchful of the children.

—◄o►—

"Sam has seizures, Hanh," Herb explained. "Sometimes you will hear noises." Lifting a threatening fist, he pretended to pound the common wall adjoining their apartments . . . "blam, blam, blam!"

"Sam is sick," he told the family. "Sometimes he hollers, but he won't hurt you. Do you understand?"

I watched their eyes for the familiar light. It wasn't there.

I glanced at Herb . . . "How else can we explain this?"

"Look it up in 'The Book,'" he said.

Herb leafed through the pages, then, held up The Book for Bi and Hanh to read in Vietnamese.

A sudden pang shot through me.

"Herb, look at them. They're scared. Maybe the definition is a jumble of superstition!"

"You might be right," he said. "That travel book said some believe people can injure them by casting spells."

Whether the family was superstitious, however, was not the issue at the moment. Instilling trust in their present living situation was. We could work on superfluous things later.

I paged through The Book to 'hurt.' Bi hung over my shoulder, and Hanh slipped by her side. Looking squarely at them, I said, "Do not go close to Sam, and "Sam . . . will . . . not . . . hurt . . . you."

I enunciated the words slowly, pointing in the direction of his apartment.

Bi cowered back and grabbed Hanh's arm.

It quickly became evident that they distrusted my judgment.

"Hanh," I tried again. "Sam will not hurt Hanh and Bi or My and Tuan. But stay away from him. Sam is not well."

The forlorn couple nodded their heads soberly, their emotional reaction doubting the cerebral data we fed them.

Bi rose and led us into the children's room. Stepping past the closet, she pointed toward the ceiling where a garret hole gaped, uncovered. Her enormous eyes spoke for her.

"Sam come here?" she asked.

"No, Bi!" I exclaimed. "The hole in the ceiling is your attic."

I showed her the pulley that lowered the steps and gestured them through an explanation. "You put your moving boxes up here. Sam cannot come here."

Tenuously satisfied with our lame-like efforts, we left the Nguyen household.

Herb revved up the Plymouth and grinned a half smile in the darkness. Arching his brow, he said, "I bet they're glad they have a telephone now."

10
Chung

Lonely for Home

Three times I pounded on the door. Chung did not answer. Suddenly, the door latch opened, and a man with high cheekbones and broad forehead appeared.

"Please . . . come in," Chung stammered uncomfortably.

Evidently embarrassed, he grasped his gaping shirt together at the top, bowed slightly, and then, he retreated. He politely closed the door while we waited in the foyer. Adam and MiRan shuffled from one cramped corner to another in the tiny foyer. Soon, my patience wore thin as their personalities collided.

"Mom, where is he?" Adam asked. He looked a bit ridiculous with his oversized jacket hugging his shoulders. He liked wearing it to accommodate the fitful Ohio weather.

I checked my watch. Five minutes had lapsed since we arrived. Where was Chung? Perhaps he wasn't accustomed to people visiting his apartment. Maybe he felt a compulsion to rearrange the room in more orderly fashion when company showed up at the door.

He should see my house! I thought, chuckling.

Chung visited Hanh and Bi on several occasions after they settled in their apartment. Through them, we learned that the veterinarian was, indeed, a very depressed man—lonely for his wife and son who were still in Vietnam. He nightmared for months that they might be dead because of his affiliation with Americans.

As months stretched into years, he and a friend resettled together but, eventually, the friend moved to another city, leaving Chung alone. Trained in medicine, he was highly intelligent, but under-employed at a local factory because of his difficulty with English. Night after night he studied to pass his language exam. Only by passing it could he legally practice his trade in America.

Hanh informed us that Chung corresponded regularly with another friend in France. Through this friend, after three and a half years of separation, Chung's wife finally learned of his whereabouts. She and their son were managing, she said. They lived in a compound with her aunt in Ho Chi Minh City.[8] Working as a midwife, she made a meager, but adequate living.

Chung must have wanted desperately to encircle his arms around the woman he married, to smell the scent of lotus[9] in her silken hair. He probably longed to hear her gentle voice and caress her soft *ao dai*.[10] But most of all, he surely wanted to gaze into her almond eyes, inebriated with the reality that they were finally together.

Why didn't he answer her letters? Perhaps he feared that, given his experiences, it would be more than he, or they, could bear. In his travels he witnessed horrors . . . wholesale killings, the ruthless murders of women and children, dead mothers with babies still at the breast. In hospital camps he treated soldiers, some of them his cohorts. They lay there moaning, their faces mangled, limbs dismembered, minds deranged—the horrible fallout of war.

And the orphans—Oh God, the orphans! After every battle, hundreds roamed the countryside like packs of animals with no place to call home.

At one point in Chung's itinerary, he accidentally stumbled upon a group of boys in a swamp sixty kilometers southwest of Saigon. When they invited him into their compound, Chung removed his boots and waded up to his calves to reach the clearing they called home. The boys numbered at least two hundred. As far as he could tell, no adult was on the premises to care for them.

Ingeniously, the boys had lashed rafts and placed them over the forest floor. In this way, they elevated their living quarters up off the swampy ground. At the far side of the makeshift structure stood two steel drums found near a bombed-out military compound.

Embarrassed by the muddy path Chung had to use to get there, several boys brought containers of murky water to wash his feet. Chung later learned that this was their drinking water.

When he returned to Saigon, he did not forget the orphaned boys.

8 Ho Chi Minh City, formerly 'Saigon'

9 In Buddhism, the lotus symbolizes beauty, prosperity and fertility. It is often used to describe feminine beauty, especially the eyes. http://www.theflowerexpert.com/content/miscellaneous/flowers-and-religion

10 'ao dai' is a traditional Vietnamese dress

Pounding the streets, he scoured the city until he found a Catholic priest willing to care for them.

-◄o►-

With a wave of his hand, Chung invited us into his apartment and gestured for us to sit down. Placing himself discreetly to the right, with my children nearby where I could watch them, the effect mesmerized Adam and MiRan. They sat stoically, their eyes scrutinizing the apartment.

I began. "Dr. Chung, you know we're trying to get Bi and Hanh's baby out of Vietnam?"

"Yes, yes, I know," he said, his head bobbing in little spurts.

"The State Department contacted us last week about family reunification for Bi and Hanh's infant daughter. Unfortunately, Bi and Hanh must wait two years before they can apply for citizenship here. They have to do that first before they can apply for their baby."

Chung nodded his head.

Fishing in my purse, I produced several documents.

"Chung, You've been in the states for four years now. We understand you have a wife and son still in Vietnam. Are you aware that you don't have to wait any longer, that family reunification is possible for you? You can apply for them now!"

He cupped his head in his hands, as if to say, *So she has come to talk about this?*

Chung's Asian stoicism braced him, as his eyes stared at the floor. His posture cried out to me that I had opened an old and painful wound. In my haste for him to decide, I had leaped into his innermost soul without his prior permission. In his silent demeanor, I could almost hear him cry, "Jeanne, you have no right to be here!"

Realizing my intrusion, I felt a need to rationalize the gap between our social relationship and his private concerns with legitimate reasons to be there. Clearing my throat, I slipped from one delicate stepping stone to another. "Chung, I had a conversation with Mr. Sponga at the Refugee Task Force. He said Vietnam is open to negotiations now. If you apply for permanent residency, we can help you."

I rattled through the procedure our government would initiate to bring his wife to Bryan. "Chung, she can come now."

He froze in his stoic position and swallowed hard. "Chean," he said, "I lif' always wit' a very big lump in my throat. I work all day, study English all night. I must do this or lose my mind."

"May we help you work through the process, Chung?"

"No," he protested in a raspy whisper. "I afraid for my family."

Chung staid his emotions in the tense air, filling it with extraneous topics. He spoke rapidly in a thick accent, so much so, that I fathomed only parts of what he was trying to tell me. Finally, he came full circle.

"I telephone my friend in Ame'dica many times," he sighed. "He tell me North Vietnam, 'shoot, shoot, shoot'!" The bitter words strained from his lips, as he looked to my eyes for understanding.

Despair, it seemed, was deeply ingrained in Chung's psyche. The horror of war had taken its toll, and he could not fathom a future beyond it. He was browbeaten to the point of distraction, not only by the enemy, but by himself for all that happened. Sadly, he no longer had the energy to jump those hurdles, even in the interest of connecting with his family.

Anything I could say to Chung, at this point, seemed woefully inadequate, but I decided to make one last effort. We needed to act immediately if anything was to happen. The amnesty provided by both countries was a highly unusual opportunity.

"Dr. Chung, please listen carefully. There's something important I must share with you."

He nodded.

"In February of this year The U.S. State Department announced that Vietnam was easing its policy for family reunification. As a result, many are leaving Vietnam and migrating to America to be with their loved ones. The time is ripe now, Chung. Your wife and son can come, but you must apply for their passage."

I pressed again, looking at his eyes for understanding.

"Don't you want them here, Chung?"

The anguished expression on his face told me that he, indeed, craved their presence, but his experiences during the war led him, beyond anything we in the West could fathom, to doubt the truth of the Communists' claims.

"Chean, I cannot. They maybe will die."

I dropped my head in defeat. He wasn't even going to try.

Was Chung's reticence due to his cultural background? Or did he rightly distrust the Communists for whom I had no schema?

I never knew what Chung thought, only that he was lonely. He locked himself in his own private prison and promptly discarded the key. He never applied for his wife and son. They were alive and well, and that was enough for the present.

11
Freedom to Give

A job, at last!

How long 'til Hanh gets job, Daddy?"
Hanh's persistent question troubled Earl during their first few months together. Freedom for Hanh meant getting a job and self-sufficiency.

A few weeks later, he was thrilled when the church found him a position at Ohio Art. Known for producing toys, especially their globes and the popular Etch-a-Sketch, the company claimed to be the world's largest toy factory under one roof. It seemed an appropriate atmosphere for Hanh to build his confidence.

That morning before he left for work, Earl dialed him at 6:00.

"Ha-llo," Hanh's voice strained into the phone.

Earl was surprised. "Hanh, you're up? How are you?"

"Veddy goot. T'ank you, Daddy."

"Are you getting ready for work?"

"Yeah!"

"Good! We'll see you for supper tonight, okay?"

No one, except one who had lost everything, could experience the pride that Hanh felt as he walked out the door with his lunch box that morning.

When he arrived at work, the premises swallowed him up as if to say, 'You, Mr. Nguyen, are no longer a man without a country. You are now a World Citizen!'

◄◦►

Two weeks later, Hanh called Earl, distraught.

"Daddy, I work. Why no money?"

Hanh's comment surprised Earl. Hanh was supposed to get a paycheck that day.

"Didn't you get your check, Hanh?"

"No, Daddy, no mo-ney! Man gif' me little. . ." he took time from the phone to banter with Bi, and then returned, ". . . little paper."

"Hanh," Earl drooled waggishly, "that's your check! Everybody gets paid with a check."

"No money, Daddy! How I buy food, my family?"

All Hanh received from his boss was a worthless slip of paper. Why couldn't Daddy understand that?

Earl slid his hand across his forehead, frustration tightening his muscles. How could he explain the American monetary system to a man who barely knew English? The situation might have been comical, had he not been pressed for an answer.

"Hanh, did the boss give you a paper? "Yes or no?"

"Yeah," Hanh answered.

"That is your money, Hanh. It's a check. Tomorrow Daddy will take you to the bank. You can give your paper to the bank, and bank will give you money. Understand?"

Silence met Earl on the other end of the line. Finally an exasperated answer seeped through.

"No un'erstand."

"OK, Hanh. I'll come over after work to help you."

The call ended with a slow, depressed sigh. Hanh thought to himself, "Why did Americans complicate the monetary system by giving worthless pieces of paper when what one really needed was money?

The system seemed preposterous to him.

◄〇►

Each day I beat a path to our mailbox, looking for news from Congressman Latta.

Though we had requested forms from Immigration and Naturalization in Washington, DC, our hands were tied until they waved the waiting period for Bi and Hanh's baby.

One month passed, then, two. The preposterously long wait seemed a malicious thieving of time.

Finally, one sultry day in June, there it lay ...sandwiched between the electric bill and The Bryan Times.

Impulsively, I ripped the envelope open. A folded letter fell out with bureaucratic insignia. It read . . .

Dear Dr. and Mrs. Smith:

"This letter regards the status of the Hanh and Bi Nguyen

family which, per your communication with me, left an infant daughter in Vietnam. I had hoped for a more encouraging report but regret to inform you that the two-year residency requirement before the family may apply for adjustment of status to that of permanent residents cannot be waived. Until that time, we cannot complete the requested transaction."
Sincerely yours,
Delbert L. Latta
House of Representatives
United States of America

My heart sank.

Dropping the missive onto our porch, I jammed my hands deep in my pockets. Stomping aimlessly outside, I headed for the garden, Treading from beans to melons to corn, but attending to none of them, my mind was light years away searching for an answer. Finally, in exasperation, I turned and retreated to the house, my frustration too painful to work itself out of my system.

Back inside, I forced myself into the office and shuffled madly through a stack of papers. Finally, my eyes lit upon it, an address for the United Nations High Commissioner of Refugees.

Sliding letterhead into the typewriter, I formulated my thoughts and started to peck the keys. The letter wrote itself. In minutes, I defined the situation and made the request for humanitarian parole for the Nguyen baby.

A half hour later, we pulled up to the post office. Adam stretched his arm out the window and dropped the envelope in the mailbox.

MiRan's petite nose formed a perfect circle against the back windowpane as we pulled away. The letter would go out that evening.

All we had to do again was . . . *wait!*

◄o►

"Daddy, why people give letters in church . . . why so many letters?"

Hanh asked the question during the service, oblivious to people sitting nearby. He had been eyeing the offering envelopes for weeks, wondering about their contents.

Earl chuckled to himself, then, put a brake on his laughter by facing straight ahead to discourage Hanh from further conversation.

After the service, Herb asked Hanh and Bi to join him in the narthex to greet our members. Though the petite Asian couple waded through countless handshakes, they received a full range of hugs and "how-are-yous" from our members. They were becoming an integral part of our church family.

The vicissitude of their presence with us seemed to be shifting from the mountainous Malaysian landscape to the flatlands of Ohio. And we were metamorphosing with them in a sense of communion.

◄o►

The following Sunday, Earl and Billie drove the family home after the service.

Hanh asked, "Daddy, why people put letters . . . "

". . . in the offering?" Earl laughed, finishing Hanh's sentence. "Those aren't letters, Hanh. People put money in the envelopes!"

Hanh looked confused. "Money?"

"Yes, money," Earl retorted. "Money helps the church pay its bills. It, also, helped us bring you to America."

Hanh and Bi engaged in conversation. Their punctuated chatter filled the Kornrumpf car, interrupted only by occasional parental commands, in English, for My and Tuan to "be goot!"

◄o►

Moments later, Hanh's head appeared over the front seat.

"Daddy, Hanh work now. My wife say we have letters, too?"

Earl's eyes widened. He glanced at Billie on the passenger side.

"Yes, Hanh," he said, "you may have 'letters,' but only if you want to give money to the church."

"I like, Daddy. My wife say she like, too."

Bi smiled, and Hanh flushed with pride that they could give back to the church that made their sponsorship possible.

This Buddhist family, weekly, for as long as they lived among us, contributed to the life of the Christian church as a sign of their gratitude.

How many Christians would do the same?

The above comment was meant to be read twice.

12
Cam o'n ong . . . Thank You

In Their Struggle for Identity, They Stumble over Happiness.

Several times per week, we drove to the Nguyens' apartment to see how they were faring. As their English skills improved, we asked about their lives in Vietnam and their extended families. More often than not, their baby came up in conversation. They knew Church World Service was working on their behalf, as well as the U.S. State Department.

One Sunday afternoon, after the children went out to play, we engaged in our usual chatter. At one point, Hanh looked askance at Bi, as if asking her consent for something in a non-verbal language.

Shortly, he disappeared into a bedroom and returned with a duffle bag, the one they brought from Vietnam. Positioning himself in an overstuffed chair, he rummaged through its contents.

In minutes, a gleam of light crossed Hanh's face, as he handed a tiny box to me.

"Here," he said. "This for you, Chean . . . becau' you try get our baby back."

A small emerald box nestled in his hands, its elongated shape suggesting something exotic. The look in Hanh's eyes told me I dared not refuse it.

My arms protruded, almost robotically, to receive it.

Hanh carefully placed the cache in my hands. Bi's eyes darted from the elixir to my expression, awaiting my reaction.

I felt a hot flush burn across my face and tried to hold back my emotions. That duffle bag contained everything they owned when they arrived in Toledo. This gift was not a trinkets-for-pearls exchange, but rather, a sacrifice analogous to a cherished heirloom. It seemed a gift far out of proportion with anything we had done to help them.

My fingers fumbled with the box. Loosening its lid, I drew out a tiny flacon of amber green. Shaped like a pentagon, it had a paper with instructions.

Hanh mused at the hieroglyphs. "This Hong Kong, this Chinese, this Malaysia, this English," he said, pointing to the translations. "I cannot read."

Dầu gió xanh con Ó, also known as Fong Yeow Cheng, is a medicated oil with a pleasant scent, available at www.enjoy-vietnam.com.

I examined the precautions carefully. Several illustrations depicted persons in varying states of agony. Flipping the tiny pages, my eyes lit on the English version of this unusual elixir.

"*Dầu gió xanh con Ó*", also known as (Fong Yeow Cheng) is prepared from a German formulae with high quality medicines and fragrant essences to give prompt and lasting relief. Its pleasant scent makes it the first medicated oil in history which can be utilised as a perfume."[11]

Unscrewing the cap, a fragrance of eucalyptus whiffed across the room. I studied its specifications on an insert in the package. Translated into several languages, it claimed to be an antidote for flu, the common cold, and a number of other ailments. I fondled the bottle, inspecting the squiggly Chinese characters and its unique pentagon shape. It smacked of a healing elixir and felt comfortable in the palm of my hand . . . an extravagant pleasure from an exotic land overflowing with narcissus.

I closed my eyes for a moment. I liked this gift. I truly, truly liked it.

---

11 See www.enjoy-vietnam.com .

More than embarrassed, I dared not show it visibly. Instead, I swallowed hard and extended my hand to Bi and Hanh. They grabbed and clasped it, acknowledging my gratitude.

Eucalyptus, I surmised, *just another way of saying 'thank you'. And so are little green peppers.*

I felt as though my head had been anointed.

━◄○►━

Dragons and fairies constitute part of ancient Vietnamese lore. In time, we learned that, in past generations, they coexisted with superstition and evil spirits.

Little My wore a charm of nickel gray around her neck. We asked Bi why.

"When My is baby," she explained, "My get veddy sick. We take her to man . . . he do like this."

Bi folded the palms of her hands, as if in prayer. "Man do long time," she added. "My get well. He say 'My wear this . . . 'neck-lace', I t'ink you say. She not get sick again.'"

Bi delighted in sharing this story, which gave Billie and me an opportunity to share the tenets of our faith, as well. We discussed religion at great length that day. As far as we could tell, their branch of Buddhism adhered to a belief in a Supreme Being and compassion toward humanity. They, also, believed, she said, that the human soul is reborn from one moment to the next and never dies.

━◄○►━

After months of struggling with these thoughts, I finally came to the conclusion that, given the myriad of interpretations of the Supreme Power around the globe by millions of Christians, Jews, Buddhists, Muslims, Shinto, and other religious traditions, perhaps in the final analysis, all one can do is to humbly admit that we human beings have myopic vision. In reality, 'God is God is God is God', and much of the rest is the overlay of our cultural understandings'.

As for myself, I reaffirmed the faith of my baptism . . . that Jesus Christ is, was, and always will be the Lodestar of my life. In the meantime, Bi and Hanh needed space. They would make their own decision.

━◄○►━

Genealogical bloodlines were of utmost importance to the family. "When man die, he haf' son," Hanh said. "If he not have son, he not happy."

Herb's seminars on the world religions shed light on the import of family lineage in Buddhism. Thus, we gleaned what Hanh was saying: 'The first son must pay homage to his dead ancestors to spare the deceased person's spirit the horror of wandering homeless forever. If a man dies without a son, his family lineage will be broken.'

Hanh's eyes sparkled with the wisdom of an ancient culture deeply ingrained. "If old man 'n' don' like somet'ing, I say, 'I don' like', and ef'rybody listen. But young man can not say, so I mus' listen Uncle."

Finally, we came full circle. For centuries, their culture had ingrained in them a reverence for one's elders. That's why Hanh and Bi venerated Billie and Earl as their American parents.

Bi continued. "In Vietnam, family veddy important. Hanh's aunt unhappy wit' me, but I mus' do ef'ryt'ing she say. Because she old, I mus' do."

Hanh paused, then set his jaw squarely.

"Uncle very luf me," he said, "but Uncle in Calnifornya." His eyes betrayed his calm exterior.

Bi interrupted. "Uncle goot to Hanh, me, children, but Uncle wife angry."

"Uncle gif' money . . . we go boat, Malaysia," Hanh explained. "In camp we lif' wit' Uncle. Vietnam say Uncle help me. Vietnam don' like."

Bi intercepted. "My sick, veddy sick. In hospital, one week. Uncle wife not want gif' money for My in hospital. No medicine, My will die."

Hanh picked up where she left off. "But Uncle veddy love us. He pay fifteen dollah to hospital for My. Uncle wife angry."

Bi shuffled her head left, then right. "She talk, talk, talk—talk too much to ef'rybody. Hanh 'n' I cry, cry. We 'shamed.

Bi's vehement admission told me they had been disparaged by Uncle's wife in the presence of friends and others. The psyche can only tolerate so much before it retreats, much like a rabbit fearing for its life withdraws into its enclave.

Not having other alternatives, the couple endured her ridicule. When they made the decision to distance themselves from Uncle's family and come to Bryan, they endured reprehension, not only from his aunt, but also, from their countrymen.

Months later in America, they took a giant leap to freedom when they resettled in Bryan.

Bi's countenance fell as we discussed their conundrum. Neither she nor Hanh could exonerate the aunt's behavior. They felt badly about severing their relationship with Uncle, but until the problem with Aunt was resolved, they needed space for healing. Thus, they remained with us.

"Uncle' wife not goot our family," Bi said. "We afraid My die."

They looked at us, aching for understanding. A rueful determination tugged at the corners of Hanh's mouth.

"We in Bryan now," he said. "We have house. I work, buy food, pay rent, have doctor for my family. Mommy, Daddy, luf' us. Herb, Chean, luf' us. Church people luf' my family. Bryan our home now!"

An unwavering modulation undergirded Hanh's pronouncement. His high cheekbones set off his eyes as his raspy voice softened to a whisper. "We lif' here now. We happy here," he said.

What we, as their sponsors, had hoped for was coming to fruition. The family sensed our compassion. Regaining self esteem, they were reconstructing their lives in their new environment. And in their struggle for personhood, they had found contentment.

Hanh said so himself.

13

The Rosebud

Attempts to Retrieve 'Little One Lost'

Bi and Hanh's sprightly four-year-old could have easily passed for a mischievous fairy in Vietnam.

"MiWan can stay and play wit' us?" My whooped triumphantly.

She cautiously awaited her mother's favorable response before springing into a fit of glee, while clamoring for her approval.

When Bi and I consented, MiRan whooped as though she had won a championship. Together, the girls and little Tuan scrambled into the play room.

Bi was delighted. She liked pleasing me, her American sister, and she felt a special kinship with MiRan, likely because she was Asian.

"I luf MiRan, Adam, same-same My and Tuan," she confided one afternoon. "You, Chean, same-same my sister, Vietnam."

Flattered at her kind words, I felt honored and humbled.

Bi knew she would probably never see her siblings again but, in a round-about way, our family situations mirrored each other's. Like Bi, Herb and I lived far from our homes, five hundred miles East in Pennsylvania, so we seldom saw our families. Although the freedom to visit existed, we only had that privilege once a year during Herb's vacation. Thus, Bi and I became constant companions.

At three o'clock I returned for MiRan, Adam traipsing by my side. A self-conscious seven-year-old, he was grateful Bi had not invited him. An afternoon free from his pesky little sister meant playing unattended with Herb's coin collection, a few exotic foreign coins, plus penny books dating from the early 1900s. For three hours non-stop, Adam peered intently into a magnifying glass, happy to be home without her.

When we returned to pick up MiRan, Bi whisked me into her kitchen, revealing a platter heaped with chicken. She smiled at me.

"I cook for Herb, Jeanne, Adam, MiRan! You eat at my house tonight?"

"Oh, Bi, we can't," I lamented, not wanting to burden her. More than once in recent weeks we had witnessed an unnatural flush in her cheeks, combined with complaints of an inflamed stomach. During these times a terrible lethargy seemed to seize her, and she spent afternoons in bed. Billie and I secretly wondered whether her problem was psychosomatic, for Bi admitted to both of us that, though days with the children kept her busy, her nights turned into agony as she lay awake with insomnia thinking about their baby.

"You watched MiRan today. You are tired now," I told her.

"No," she protested. She didn't want my sympathy. "You come, supper. I like!"

Bi's cheeks flushed like those of a woman in charge of her household. Her life was finally normalizing, and she could play the gracious hostess.

◄○►

Back at the parsonage, I called Herb to check his schedule.

"Sure, we can go. What time?"

"I told her 6:00."

Trying on the thought for size, he asked, "Will our kids like the Vietnamese food? What if they're persnickety?"

Turning on my heel, I yelled to the top of the stairs.

"Adam and Ronnie! We're going to Hanh and Bi's for dinner tonight!"

They scrambled down the steps, taking them two at a time. Tumbling over each other, they collided, landing at the bottom in an entangled mass. MiRan threw her head back in laughter as Adam scuffled upright on his feet.

"What did ya' say, Mom?" he rambled, diverting his attention to MiRan's pony tail, which he yanked maliciously.

"Mom, Adam's buggin' me!" she scolded, as she kicked him in the ankle. The rivalry between the two could not be resolved and possibly never would be.

My right brow arched in business-like pursuit. "I have something to ask you."

Both stiffened to attention. Adam's eyes danced with mischief as they darted in the direction of his little sister, his pincher fingers perched for an attack.

"Whatcha' want, Mom?" he asked.

MiRan echoed Big Brother. "Yeah, what?"

Adam flattened his arms robotically at his sides. Though he didn't move from his about-face position, his eyes wandered askance in their sockets as he flexed his pincher finger in MiRan's direction.

He wasn't finished with his kid sister yet.

"Cut out the nonsense, you two!"

Then, crossing my arms, I added, "We're going to Hanh and Bi's for dinner this evening. I'm not sure what Bi's having, but it might be something unusual. If you don't like the food, I have a suggestion."

"Yeah?" Adam retorted.

"Yeah?" MiRan parroted.

"I can make you sandwiches before we leave so you won't get hungry."

Adam's tongue slurped, savoring the thought of food, especially with dinner approaching.

"Peanut butter, Mom?"

"Sounds good," I quipped.

His eyes glanced sideways toward his little sister as if to say, 'Hey! Mom's in a good mood today!' Chuckling to myself, I spread two large slices of bread with their favorite delicacy.

—<o>—

The aromatic scent of soy greeted us at the door. Bi was queen in her kitchen now, with Hanh her lead assistant. Together they tossed Ramen noodles with stir fried veggies, bits of chicken, and ginger root. The spicy fragrance convinced me that my children would like this meal if only they would taste it.

Bi recited the menu as she arranged the feast on the table. Brushing a dark wave from her forehead, she seemed exceptionally vibrant tonight, like a flower in first bloom. I studied her expression, and then, somewhat embarrassed, noticed she was watching me.

She smiled shyly as we joined our hands to pray, just as they had done with Billie and Earl each evening.

My offered grace unabashedly, parroting the prayers from the Kornrumpf home.

"Dear Got, t'ank you for da food, an' Hub an' Chean an' Ah-dam an' MiWan. T'ank you for Mommy an' Daddy an' Tuan an' My an' Gwamma an' Gwampa."

My's eyes darted around the room, satisfied she forgot no one.

"Ah-man," her chirpy voice concluded.

To my surprise, Adam and MiRan attacked the food—*Meo Sau*, Bi called it. The kids even asked for seconds.

At one point, My shouted, "Look at Ah-dam . . . ha, ha, ha!"

Adam was slurping long squiggly noodles, curling down past his chin.

REFUGEES: *A Family's Search for Freedom and a Church That Helped Them Find It*

Bi cooking *Meo-Sau*

The seasonings were exceptional, and in our son's determination to down them hurriedly, he anchored a mouthful with his wide toothy grin. Long strands of wiggly pasta emerged from his mouth, bearding his chin. He looked like a little old Chinaman swallowing his cheeks to suck them in.

Our reaction to Bi's cuisine delighted her. The fact that she and Hanh could give something back that we enjoyed enhanced their self-esteem.

After the meal, we carried the dishes to the sink. I leaned against the kitchen door while Bi buried her arms up to her elbows in suds. I felt ridiculous watching her and dove for a dish towel once too often.

"No!" she shouted, grabbing my shoulders with her sopping hands. She swung me around and gave me a boot out the door, then, firmly drove her statement home . . . "I do! You sit dow"!"

Then, as if to apologize, she added. "I want t'ank you veddy much."

Finally, I understood. To insist even one more time would have been the ultimate insult for the little Asian woman. I knew how to give, but didn't know how to receive.

◀○▶

After the meal, we settled in the living room.

Herb asked, "Hanh, what is your baby's name?"

Bi seated herself next to him, while I deposited myself in a chair, eager for his answer.

Hanh's dark eyes filled with tenderness. "Ngoc My," he answered, then added, "an' we haf' two babies die." He rattled the ice cubes in his glass to deflect us from the hurt in his eyes.

"And that is very painful for you?" Herb asked.

Hanh glanced at us sadly and cleared his throat. "Yeah."

I looked deep into his countenance, at the high cheekbones and penetrating eyes. This young father, at twenty six years, had more on his plate than we could fathom. In Vietnam, he had experienced, not only the loss of their baby, but also, the horrors of war.

Though able to start again, the refreshing burst of energy Hanh found in Bryan was fraught with painful memories, not only of his homeland, but of their baby left behind. Just one of these would have been more than enough, but his loss was exponential.

I tried to lighten the mood but didn't know if I could. Still, I had to try. My eyes fixed on Hanh, determined to communicate.

Tentatively, I began. "Hanh, about 'Ngoc My', your baby in Vietnam, we are trying to bring her to America."

Hanh studied my expression. "I know," he said.

"Measuring the amount of hope we dared mete out, I continued. "We wrote a letter to Mr. Latta,[12] a worker in our government."

Hanh nodded. He knew all too well what 'government' meant.

"Mr. Latta said we must wait for your baby for two years. Then, we wrote a second letter to another government official. He told us he'll try to get your baby sooner . . . if such is possible."

---

12 A former member of the United States House of Representatives, Delbert Latta was a Republican from Ohio. https://en.wikipedia.org/wiki/Del_Latta.

Hanh leaned into the conversation, hanging onto my words.

Shrugging my shoulders, I added, "but we must wait for his guidance now."

Hanh looked deep into my eyes to read the meaning there. I tried to smile to let him know we were trying, for even the slightest tinge of hope glimmers in the nighttime of despair.

Hanh nodded slowly. He understood.

◄O►

Sultry afternoons climaxed in refreshing rains that cooled the Ohio countryside and summer began in earnest. Ripping open the letter delivered just moments before, I read . . .

Dr. and Mrs. Smith:

I am responding to your recent query concerning family reunification for Mr. and Mrs. Hanh Nguyen's infant daughter.

The U.S. and Vietnamese governments have not yet established diplomatic relations. Unfortunately, thousands of Vietnamese are requesting traveling privileges to reunite with their families in the United States.

I regret to inform you that until such time as diplomatic relations between the two governments are established, this Service is unable to render any assistance to citizens of Vietnam. However, in the event the child is able to depart Vietnam, this Service will render her all possible assistance within the parameters of outstanding laws and regulations.

Sincerely,
Carl J. Wack, Jr.
Associate Commissioner
U.S. Department of Justice

I clenched the arms of my chair and shook my head in frustration.

"No!" I whimpered, "No!"

The gossamer web on which we had placed our hope had frayed and ruptured. Rage took hold within, and denial turned to anger.

I thrust the letter on the desk and sank into a chair.

"They regret, they regret, they regret! Is that all that they can say?" My head fell limp in my arms, discouraged. "Oh, that governments had human hearts like people!"

I shuddered. I had to get out of the house. The air was too close, too tight to breathe.

I raced outside, releasing tension into the atmosphere. The children joined me, and we hopped over puddles of teary sky together. Steam rose from the hot, wet pavement, leaving tracks behind us. I had to forget, for a while, if only my heart would let me.

We frolicked around the church yard, stopping to rest only when winded. Cool droplets of water tickled our toes in blades of emerald grass. We checked the tulips, long withered on their stems.

Our sprightly MiRan beckoned me to come over.

"Mommy, looka' this one!" she chortled.

Slipping to her side, I knelt between the children and peered into the bushes. There, a Pyrocantha showcased scarlet berries blushing with color. Laden with droplets of light, its soft petals gently unfurled, revealing intrinsic beauty.

"Mommy, can you see the little one?" she asked.

Her observant eyes regarded a single bud that had yet to open, its sepals tightly bound around the beauty of the blossom inside its purple carcass.

My lips parted and I whispered, "Come, little one, come out of your cocoon. Why can't we reach you, little Ngoc My, in a far-off land?"

A ruthless gardener might have plucked the straggly branch from the living vine, yet a touch of life was there, and the roots could nourish it still.

I dared not pluck it.

I had more hope than that.

14

The Book

English lessons, Laubach, and 'hot dogs'

"This . . . is . . . an . . . apple," Wilma underlined the words of the picture for Bi and Hanh with her finger. "Say, 'apple'!"

"Apfle. Thes . . . es . . . an . . . apfle," they repeated after her.

Wilma continued. "This . . . is . . . a . . . plate."

Oversized pictures with words printed beneath them were propped, one at a time, in front of Hanh and Bi to help them connect physical objects with English vocabulary.

At first, our teachers, Florence and Wilma, created their own curricula for the family. Only later did we learn about the streamlined Laubach method of teaching English as a second language. One Saturday several of us took off for Fort Wayne to learn how to teach it. After a day of intense instruction, we piled into the car to head home.

"But we've been teaching Laubach all along!" Wilma insisted.

To our advantage, Florence and Wilma's combined years of experience teaching in local schools had uncovered basic universal truths about the way children learn.

◄◦►

"Po-ta-to. This . . . is . . . a . . . potato," Wilma continued, archly. A former missionary in Nigeria, she was a demanding teacher who asked for her students' best and usually got it.

"Po-ta-to. Thees . . . es . . . a . . . potato," Bi echoed.

Placards with vocabulary words were used to teach the family English every Saturday. Eventually, the cards were flipped so frequently that their edges grew ragged from wear. Even The Book took a beating when its binding began to break.

"Wilma," Florence chastised one day. "This dictionary belongs to Chung, but I'm embarrassed to return it."

Florence fondled the tattered leaves between her hands. When a sheaf of pages slid to the floor and scattered out of order, little My scrambled to retrieve them.

Wilma retorted, "The dictionary can be replaced, Florence. Put in an order for two."

"Two? At fifteen dollars a piece?"

Wilma peered authoritatively over her glasses in their improvised classroom. "Sure. One for them and one for Chung. How else can they learn English?"

Florence's precise diction gave way to a relaxed chuckle. "Well, I suppose if the family is using it, the broken-down dictionary is evidence of our success!"

Wilma's eyes lit up. "That's right!"

She pounded her fist on the table and exclaimed, "If that dictionary weren't falling apart, we wouldn't be doing our job!"

English meant survival for the family.

◄o►

Bi (left) and Hanh study English on a daily basis.

Bi quickly comprehended the flow of the English language, strangely different from her native tongue. We attempted to learn a bit of Vietnamese, but the eighty-nine letters of their alphabet, including their vowels with diacritical markings served only to confuse us. Because Vietnamese is a tonal language, a word can have up to six different meanings, depending upon the tone with which it is pronounced.

Doing a bit of research, we learned that tones depend largely upon vowels. The letters 'a' and 'o', for example, could be written and pronounced eighteen different ways, the word, 'ma', being a prime example. The phrasebook overwhelmed us when we realized 'ma' could be a ghost, a mother, a tomb, a rice seedling, or even a ceremonial paper burned at a funeral.

"I think I'll stick with English," I bantered to Bi one day.

"I go to grow'ry store to-day." Bi's lips enunciated her homework syllables in consecutive order. Our pronunciation proved as difficult for her as Vietnamese was for us.

"How you say 'grow'ry', Chean?"

"Gro-sir-ee," Bi, "Gro-sir-ee," I enunciated slowly.

She listened, her head cocked to one side, and then scribbled its Vietnamese equivalent in the margin of her workbook.

"I see affles, cah-rots, let-tuss, tu-nips, 'n' cumbahs," she continued.

"Bi," I interrupted, "it's 'cu-cum-bers'. "

She did not answer promptly.

"Coo-kum-buhs," she attempted.

"Cu-cum-bers," I repeated.

Slightly agitated, she tried again. "Coo-kum-buhs."

Discouragement was not the objective of our lesson so I quickly relinquished the task to her teachers.

Another day, Bi rummaged through a stack of papers in her closet. Producing a large, poster-sized square of tagboard on which Wilma and Florence had drawn her family tree, we set to work again.

"I haf' son, Tuan, 'n' dot-ter, My," she read rather fluently. "My weah sun-soot, 'n' Tuan weah shirt 'n' fants . . ."

"Good, Bi!" I encouraged her. "Can you say 'p-p-pants' again?"

She exuded an unusual sound from her throat. "Fants," she reiterated.

Pouting my lips in a slow, deliberate puff, I said, "p, p, p. Now, Bi, you say 'p.'"

She struggled. ". . . f, f, f ."

Leafing through their phrase book, the problem became apparent. The letter 'p' did not exist in Vietnamese. These lessons were broadening my scope of semantics as much as they were hers.

Crinkling my brow, I fished for a key word on which we could focus.

"Ngoc My," I offered.

Bi's eyes opened wide. Why did I mention her baby?

I enunciated the syllables slowly for her to hear. "You write her name, 'Ngoc My,'" but when you talk about your baby, you say, 'Nyop Mae.'"

"Say . . . "Nyop," I asked again.

"'Nyop' . . . 'Nyop My,'" she reiterated.

"Nyop . . . p . . . p," I stuttered, scrutinizing her mouth for correct lip patterns.

"Nyop . . . p . . . p, 'pants'?" she shouted, surprised.

"You did it, Bi! You can say the letter, 'P'!" I whooped triumphantly.

Every little victory resulted in celebration.

Secretly, I felt a bit guilty using her baby's name for homework, but it would be one sound that Bi consolidated quickly.

◀o▶

One of the treasures in their mysterious duffle bag was a pile of English books supplied by the United Nations in Malaysia. The books appeared worn and reminded me of textbooks my mother used as a child. Stories of elves, fairies and the lucky (or not-so-lucky) children who interacted with them graced their pages.

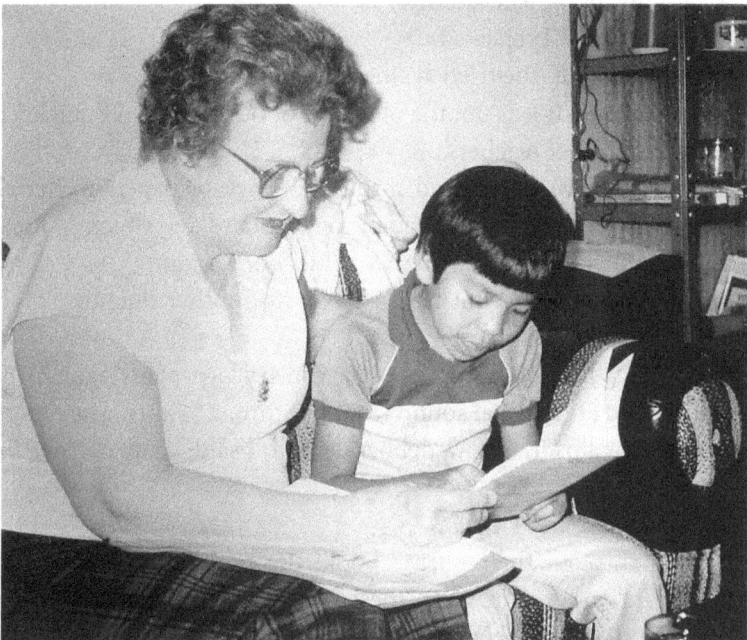

English teacher Florence listens to Tuan read.

Hanh was fortunate to have taken four weeks of English classes in Malaysia, enough to get the flow of the language and conjugate verb forms. His English improved rapidly because of his previous exposure. Later, a five week class in English as a Second Language at a local college near Bryan enabled Bi to surpass her husband.

Yet the written word and spoken languages are nebulous, at best. What seems simple to a tongue trained in cadences often resonates differently when translated in another language. Pride in the family's progress in English sometimes left me baffled when we searched for understanding of another confusing phoneme.

Many times I asked for the translation of a perplexing vocabulary word in Vietnamese, and more than once, when its meaning finally came to light, I sighed . . . 'stupid!', chastising myself for not realizing the answer.

Our church members visited Bi and Hanh's family on numerous occasions without referring to 'The Book'. They simply repeated phrases and pointed to objects to help them communicate. Using gestures, pantomime, smiles, and lots of good-spirited teasing, they enjoyed each other's company. Learning by association provided a helpful strategy for learning.

Sometimes we relaxed and exchanged tutorial roles.

"Can you teach Jeanne to count 1 to 5 in Vietnamese?" I asked them one day after our lesson.

Bi cleared her throat and smiled. "*Một*," she began.

"Moot," I mimicked lamely.

"*Hai*," she continued.

"Hi," I repeated.

"*Ba*," she went on.

"Three is '*ba*'," I said.

"*Bốn* is four," she laughed.

"Bahn!" I bellowed, teasing.

"*Năm*" is five,"

"Nahm," I mimicked after her.

Hanh's grin broadened. "Not 'nahm,' Jeanne!"

I repeated, "'Nahm'!"

Noting his displeasure, I grudgingly asked, "OK, how do I say 'Nahm' correctly?"

"'Nahm' not goot enough, Chean."

Even their children laughed at me and thought I was talking funny. "You mus' say, 'năm'!" they insisted.

"I did say, 'na-a-hm,'" I drawled.

"You did it, Chean! You say "*nãm*"!" Hanh shouted triumphantly.

Their helpless pupil sat speechless. What did I say differently?

Leaning across the table, I asked, "Why does '*nãm*' mean five, and 'Viet Nam' mean your country?"

Hanh and Bi glanced at each other, astonished. How could one not comprehend the subtle difference?

"Not 'same-same'?" I asked.

"No, not same!"

Bi's elfish grin exposed an inward pleasure at her superiority. It was great to see her 'playing teacher' in our role reversal, but not at my expense. Even little My bruised my feelings when she giggled at my efforts.

"Chean cannot count five in Vietnamese! Tuan count to ten in English! Tuan only t'ree years old. Ha, ha, ha!"

I took her in with a rueful smile.

I might have clammed into my shell altogether, had I not had to save my pride. Thus, I learned to count, one-to-ten, in Vietnamese . . . , or a reasonable facsimile thereof. My blunders did wonders for the family's morale.

As for myself, it was a lesson in humility.

◄o►

Looking back, a remarkable transformation was in process, especially when we compared the 'Hanh and Bi' we knew now with the couple we met months before on that snowy November evening.

It seemed only yesterday that Florence hummed around the countryside with Hanh and Bi, pointing out barns, trees, fields, and houses. Later, during their lessons, she jotted them down for the couple to memorize. Driving past a farm with animals, she pointed to a herd ambling into a barn and said, "Americans eat cow."

Hanh nodded his head. "Hanh, Bi eat cow."

Florence ventured, "Americans eat chicken. Does Hanh eat chicken?"

"Yeah, Hanh eat chicken."

"Do Vietnamese eat sheep?" Florence asked.

"Yeah, Vietnam eat sheep."

"Do Vietnamese eat pig?" she continued.

Hanh shook his head in the affirmative, and then had a question for her. "Vietnam . . . no eat dog. America . . . eat dog?"

Florence's eyes met his in disbelief.

"No, Hanh! Americans do not eat dog!" she exclaimed.

"You do!" Hanh insisted, without a trace of humor. "America eat dog . . . hot dog!"

Florence laughed abruptly. "Noooo!" she cried, realizing Hanh's transference. "Hot dog is not dog meat! Hot dog is pork!"

No amount of bantering could change Hanh's mind. He was thoroughly convinced that Americans ate dog, and he wanted no part of it.

At the end of the family's session that day, they wended their way through the countryside retracing the path they came. A heavy, blue streak in the westward sky hovered below the hazy sun, a sure sign of rain tomorrow. Bugs made the windshield their graveyard as Florence taxied to Billie's to take the family home.

—<o>—

Back at the Kornrumpfs, Billie rummaged in the freezer and found a pound of wieners. "Florence," she moaned, "the package doesn't say 'cow' or 'pig'. It says 'beef and pork'."

Florence looked at Hanh's suspecting eyes. "Why does Hanh think Americans eat dog?"

Hanh hesitated, and then, above the clamor of the children, he raised his voice. "Nor' Vietnam eat dog. Hot dog same, same . . . dog!'

Billie groaned.

Another aberration of the English language!

Florence persisted. "Hanh, hot dog is 'cow meat' . . . cow, Cow, COW!"

Bi's face lit up. She foraged in the toy box, leafing rapidly through a nursery rhyme book. Shuffling through its pages, she pointed to a cow, holding it up for all to see.

"Hey, diddle, diddle, the cat and the fiddle," it read.

"Billie gasped. 'The cow' jumped over the moon!

They broke into contagious laughter.

—<o>—

We became acutely aware that the English language is not all it appears to be on the surface, for just as hot dogs had nothing to do with dogs, neither did chicken pox have anything to do with chickens. However, Hanh did not laugh as lustily at the latter discrepancy as he did at the former. To his chagrin, he missed a week of work because of it.

15
The Horrors of War

Mass Exodus

After the worship service that Sunday, long tables stretched beside the pond laden with one delicacy after another. People milled around the wooded area toting picnic plates heaped with food. Children rushed hurriedly through the line to finish eating so they could wade in the water, while a group of teens splashing on a raft rowed in to sun-dry and grab some dinner. Church at Moore's pond had become an annual extravaganza.

Herb had begun the service out by the pond, as Adam and MiRan joined me. As we relaxed on an Indian blanket stretched over the dewy grass, the sun tried eagerly to shine through the balmy mist that hung over us. Droplets of rain cut the service short, but the threatening clouds soon passed over and the morning sun won the celestial debate.

A cozy atmosphere enveloped us, and after the service children begged to go swimming. Teenagers didn't ask, but jumped on in. Lines formed at the head of long tables laden with chicken, salads, and desserts. The ambiance proclaimed anew "Thanksgiving in the summer."

My eyes shifted from side to side as I wove through the crowd to find Billie. When those around her were busy, I slipped from behind to get her attention.

"Billie," I whispered, "what's wrong with Hanh?"

She lowered her head to hear me, then, looked over the sea of faces to locate the family. They must have been a safe distance away because she answered freely.

"Yesterday a letter arrived for Hanh," she said, "in care of the church."

Billie had it with her and pulled it out of her purse. I took a look at it. The exotic stamp bore the postmark of Thailand. The address had swirling diacritical marks across the envelope, running curvatures, one into the other. I read the return address:

Bi pauses with My for a photo during a
picnic at Moore's pond.

Mother Bi cuddles sleepy Tuan
at the picnic.

Nguyen Huu Manh c/o Lick Creek
Church of the Brethren Rev. Herbert
Smith Rt 4 Bryan Ohio 43506 United
States of America   4928 B8 69-834

She explained that Hanh had broken into a smile as he examined the return address, "My friend, Thailand," he said, beaming. "My friend go Thailand on boat."

Hanh had impatiently ripped the envelope open and read it like a starving man stuffing himself with potatoes.

"Then," she said, "Hanh's smile gradually faded and the light in his eyes dimmed slowly. Bi moved to his side and looked over his shoulder. She read it, too."

My eyes shifted to Bi and Hanh across the clearing. He sat fairly rigid, as though biding time in the present. Bi no longer smiled, but simply contended with the children. "What did the letter tell them?"

"The letter was from Hanh's neighbor in Vietnam. He escaped a few months ago without his family. He's single, so that's not as bad as it might have been if he were married."

Billie continued, "The friend told him that ten days after he and Bi fled, North Vietnam seized their house. Uncle's was confiscated, too."

"So that's why he looks depressed?"

"Yes. He asked if we could bring his friend here. The friend could live with them."

"But their apartment has restrictions on the number of occupants," I proffered.

"I told him that a few months ago when Chung wanted to move in."

"Chung?"

"Earl explained the restrictions of the lease to Hanh. Bi wasn't too happy about cooking for him anyway."

I crossed my arms. "I would think not. The burden would be on her."

Billie continued. "She seems more willing to take in the friend from Thailand. I imagine they learned to know him in camp."

"He might be less demanding, too," I surmised.

"If we'd apply for him, chances are he'd be in France or Canada before our request would be approved. That sounds like an excuse, but . . . "

"We'll have to think about it, though. It's always more difficult to place singles. Everybody wants families, especially those with children. They figure if they're going to the trouble for one, they might as well help several. Plus, kids are little and innocent."

I excused myself and wended my way through the crowd to find Herb. He was hunched on the bank watching Adam and MiRan splash in the water. Fully clothed, they were sopping wet, but their unrestrained merriment made me bite my tongue.

Snuggling down beside Herb in the grass, we gloated in their child-like pleasure.

I thought to myself, *Happiness is a rare commodity, delicately balanced between one's environment and the conditions within.*

We let the children squeal and laugh. We couldn't spoil their fun. They would get there sooner than they wanted. Life was hard enough.

—◄o►—

And then it happened . . . the mass exodus. Suddenly, and without warning, countries in Southeast Asia were inundated with tens of thousands of refugees fleeing Vietnam, Laos, and Cambodia. News flooded the wire daily – "Malaysian Authorities Push Vietnamese Back to Sea" and "Boat People Find Watery Graves".

Malaysia and the UPAC nations called for help on a daily basis. Prime Minister Datuk Hussein Bin Onn told, General Kurt Waldheim, the United

Nations Secretary, "Any boat carrying illegal Vietnamese immigrants that tries to enter Malaysian waters or attempts to land will be towed away."

Malaysia already harbored 76,000 refugees, most of them languishing in makeshift camps. The largest, Pulau Bidong, where Hanh and Bi found refuge, was a tiny island no more than a square mile in size. Intended to accommodate 5,000, Pulau Bidong expanded to its bursting point, with 47,000 immigrants. Living conditions bordered on wretched as a result of overcrowding.

Many Vietnamese who fled wanted to remain in-country, but were forced to leave because of their Chinese lineage. The ideological clash between Vietnamese businessmen and the Communists gave leaders of the oppression reason for elimination.

When Hussein gave his ultimatum, he reportedly coldly to the media that refugees would be cast adrift in the South China Sea. "Malaysia," he asserted, was "fully satisfied that third countries are not serious about their promise to accept them."

That same week five ramshackle boats, packed with 2,500 more refugees showed up near Kuala Besar, 250 miles northeast of the capital. Like the others, they, too, were forced back to sea.

Humanitarians world-wide rose up in indignation.

Inside sources claimed that Malaysia turned away more than 267 boats during the six months prior. With 10,000 refugees lives at stake, many were foiled into leaving because Malaysian soldiers deceived them into thinking American boats were awaiting them in international waters. The statement was untrue, but in their desperation, many sailed out with hope in their hearts . . . and found only a watery grave.

Outraged at Malaysia's ulterior tactics, The world press commented, "You can't do that." But Malaysia pointed an accusing finger and clamored, "Then YOU help, too."

My heart ached for those helpless people. I lamented Vietnam's underhanded behaviors and cringed at the neighboring countries' lack of response.

We chose not to mention the international scene to Hanh and Bi since they still had friends in Malaysia.

It didn't take long to realize what they already knew.

━◦━

A few days later, Bi and I stood over steaming pots in my kitchen straining applesauce for the freezer. Back in the playroom, the children chattered noisily as they drug a trail of toys into the living room to create a store.

MiRan served as boss of the operation, while her spritely manager, little My, piled a load of stuffed animals and miniature rocking chairs under the dining room table.

When refused the privilege of playing with them, Tuan felt like a useless ornament and ran wailing to his mother. The spat finally resolved itself when he transformed himself into a busboy and hauled a generous amount of 'merchandise' from the playroom to their cash register.

Pushing the dark waves over her forehead, Bi washed her hands and quartered the apples. As she slipped slices into the kettle, I filled the sterilized jars with sauce strained from the night before.

"In Vietnam," Bi offered, "we not do. We gro-cery effry day. Six month we lif' wit' Hanh's father. Six month we lif' wit' Hanh's Uncle."

Bi shaded her eyes pretending to look over an imaginary crowd on the sidewalk. "When we lif' Hanh's father, I sell tomato, banana outside city . . . many, many people. Little city, one t'ousand, two t'ousand people. Big city, Can Tho, four t'ousand. People ef'rywhere in street."

"In America we call that a 'market', Bi."

"Ma'ket," she repeated slowly, registering the word in her repertoire.

She continued. "I sell many, many fruit. I look in Book what you call fruit. It have no name in English. You not have that fruit in Ame'dica."

After a discourse on five types of bananas native to Vietnam, she added, "Hanh's father haf' big dogs. Hanh 'n' I veddy love dogs. When Nor' Vietnam come, they kill 'n' eat."

Her face grimaced at the thought of their pets being cannibalized by soldiers. "We haf' dogs for banana trees because no fance . . . "

I looked puzzled.

She repeated the word . . . "fance, no fance . . . so nobody steal."

'Fence', of course. That made sense.

Stretching across the table to fill another jar, I asked, "Bi, why do so many people leave Vietnam?"

"Soldiers, Chean. They kill us. No jobs. People can not work. Everything ex-pan-sive. You know what I cook, you don' like?"

Laughing, she pinched her nose, recalling their pungent fish sauce that exuded an odor too potent for our delicate western noses.

"Yeeesss," I responded, grinning.

Bi chuckled at my lack of taste, and then continued. "That what I cook you don't like . . . t'ree dollah before Nor' Vietnam come. After Nor' Vietnam come, two hundred dollah. Sugar . . . two dollah, one poun' before Nor' Vietnam; after, twenty dollah. Medicine, no can buy."

She lifted her leg and pulled at her slacks. "Fants . . . p, p, pants," she faltered, no can buy. Too ex-pan-sive. No t'read, needle, what you say? No cloth to sew . . . can not buy. When baby Ngoc My get born, no cloth to sew her clothes."

Bi finished peeling her second kettle of apples. We filled sparkling jars with sauce and tightened their lids for the canner. After lowering them into the steaming kettle, we sank into our chairs with cool glasses of tea.

"Chean," she asked, "you know about Vietnam, Malaysia, today?"

I shifted my eyes uneasily. Everything I knew was on a perfunctory level, yet her question seemed begging for a listening ear from anyone willing to take time to hear her.

Bi went on. "Malaysia say nobody can come Ame'dica now because people die."

She fingered the rim of her glass, as though she were a satellite circumambulating the globe below her.

"We haf' frien' Malaysia, Chean. They haf' new baby, little girl. They ask us send baby clothes . . . so baby look goot if she come Ame'dica."

Bi smiled at the thought of a new infant. "Hanh 'n' I want to help, but maybe soldiers steal." Her dark eyes drank in my expression.

I was dumfounded. I had no schema for this type of behavior.

Finally, I asked, "How do you know about Malaysia, Bi? Did you find a Vietnamese newspaper here?"

"Trudy gif' Hanh radio," she said. "We hear woman talk . . . from Washin'ton. She talk like me . . . in Vietnamese."

So that was it . . . they had a short wave radio!

There were no terrible secrets, after all. They knew what was happening in the world. The family was aware of everything—the raids, the bombings, the boats, the whole awful truth.

Clearly, Bi wanted to help her Vietnamese friends, but, as refugees eeking out a living, she and Hanh were not in a position to do much of anything. Even the few dollars they took from Hanh's paycheck to send to friends in camp in Thailand often didn't get through. Most likely it was intercepted.

But if Bi couldn't change the world, perhaps we could reach out to one person. "Bi," I said, "let's sew some clothes for your friend's new baby. Would you like to do that?"

Her eyes brightened as she mopped her hands on a tea towel. Then she broke into a smile. "Yeah, Chean! I like!"

I turned the spigot and a rush of water dashed over my hands. We had to get the canning jars out of the boiler.

—◄○►—

Leaning across the table, Bi carefully traced the pattern with her scissors. She lacked confidence, however, at the sewing machine's sudden spurt each time she stepped on the presser foot.

"Jeanne teach me how sew?" she asked.

"Sure, Bi," I retorted. "You sew to here . . . " (I showed her where), "and then, fold the cloth . . . " (I folded it.) " . . . and secure the zipper, like this."

I proudly displayed the neatly ironed piece to illustrate.

Bi's tightly knit brow told me she discerned the intricacies of the process. "All right," she answered.

Then, in front of my eyes, she folded the placket, stitched it down, turned the corner, flew up the other side, backstitched, lifted the zipper foot, and bit off the thread.

My eyes skimmed over her handiwork. I was not dealing with a novice!

I shot my eyes to the top of their sockets and grinned. "Where did you learn to sew, Bi?"

She smiled at me, or my ignorance, I wasn't sure which, and looked smugly pleased with her accomplishment.

"In Vietnam before Hanh 'n' Bi get marry, I sew five year in shop. I lif' wit' cousin. She have little hos-pital. She try teach me to born babies, but I cannot do."

" . . . to be a midwife?"

"Yeah, she teach me born babies. But I sick, sick . . . I cannot do," Bi laughed. "Cousin send me to shop. I learn sew. I teach five students."

My voice betrayed astonishment. "Bi, you taught five students?"

Yet there lay the proof of her expertise on the machine . . . the perfect zipper.

I fingered the metal teeth and ran the catch back and forth.

"Bi," I winked, "will you teach Jeanne to sew?"

She caught my smile between chuckles and we burst out in hearty laughter.

16
Other Churches

"Didn't you hear?"

Malaysia's refugees weighed heavily on the news in days to come. The wire printed it, airwaves intoned it, and CBS produced, "The Boat People," inundating shock waves around the world.

Hundreds of times daily Hanh and Bi's story repeated itself, as the winds of Malaysia blew their stories across the currents to us. An entire generation of their countrymen, wreaked with terror and torn by war, was dying in the bowels of the South China Sea.

In the United States President Jimmy Carter increased monthly immigration quotas to 14,000. Yet sponsors had to be found for them or they would be refused asylum.

"I wish we could sponsor again," I told Claretta one Sunday after church.

"I do, too," she said, "but we aren't ready for it yet." She was very supportive of Bi and Hanh, so I was a bit surprised at her remark.

Treading on a pebble of gravel, I kicked it to the side of the pavement. "You might be right," I continued. "True, Hanh and Bi still seem dependent, but they're paying their own bills now," I added.

Claretta's eyes flickered. "Didn't you hear about the bank?"

"No. What happened?"

Claretta apparently took Bi to the bank to make a deposit, and Bi was surprised when the bank gave her extra money . . . a whole $3.00 in interest!

Lowering her voice, Claretta stepped closer. "But when Bi learned what the deal was, that the bank was 'using her money', she whirled around and retraced her steps to the booth to get it back!"

We both laughed, but then, her smile quickly faded. "I don't think we're ready for another family yet. Hanh and Bi still have a lot to learn."

A chill fell heavily on my thoughts. I nodded in agreement.

—<o>—

Two weeks before we departed for our church denomination's annual conference in Seattle, I stood timidly by the phone. It glared at me as if daring me to lift it. If we weren't ready to sponsor yet, then who might be—other churches? Perhaps all they needed was an invitation.

Asking a church to sponsor a refugee family required courage for me. This was not a short-term undertaking. Nor would it be pleasant if the pastors were antagonistic. What if someone entangled me in a sticky debate on some political issue? I felt mentally exhausted, too tired to fight, but something had to happen. If our churches didn't step out of their comfort zones to make bold, determined stands for the world's oppressed, who else would be there for them?

I lifted the receiver. Cradling the phone against my shoulder, I paged to a list of local churches in the Yellow pages.

Reaction # 1: "No, we're not interested [click]."

Reaction # 2: "We have other financial obligations. I'm sorry, we can't do it."

And then, another . . .

Reaction #3: "Nobody in our congregation has mentioned the issue. If it's not a concern of theirs, I don't plan to initiate it."

I hug up, painfully aware of our powerlessness. The reactions were those of pastors. Didn't they read the news? Didn't they know what terrible events were unfolding on the global scene? Were they afraid of their congregations?

I wrung my hands in exasperation and paced the floor, thinking, *Relinquish the idea! Forget it!'*

But something kept nudging me. *Try again, Jeanne! You're not soliciting for a chili supper. You're saving the lives of God's children.*

My face felt chilled and drawn. I paced the floor to muster up courage, but there was none in the offing. Finally, I sank on the sofa, taut as a drawn bow, and released the tension and wept.

Feeling edgy and adolescent, I quit, angry at myself for not being more courageous.

An icy paralysis choked my throat.

What difference would it make? I thought. *A hundred years from now, we'll all be gone, and Bryan will be full of strangers. Will anything we do now be relevant then?*

I rubbed my cheeks and propped my chin in both hands. Suddenly, through the prisms in my eyes, two omniscient eyes stared back at me. A short brunette dressed in worn college sweatshirt and navy trousers mirrored a defeated woman. In my brooding face, the ghost of childhood innocence had given way to the world of experience. And then, the omniscient eyes spoke firmly to me . . .

"Jeanne, Jesus Christ is your Relevance Factor. He walks in this place today, and He'll be here a thousand years from now. He will not forget what your people are doing!"

I stared at the apparition, as though a stranger were speaking. The words were true. Action, not inaction, creates historical waves of immense proportions. Anything we did would live on in posterity in the lives of God's children.

Hopeless. Worn. Tired. That's how I felt, but now I knew what had to be done. And then I fell asleep.

A half hour later I awakened, bleary-eyed and refreshed. With a new supply of prowess, I returned to the phone.

Reaction #4: "We hadn't thought about sponsoring, but it would be good for our congregation. I'll bring it up to the board this weekend . . . "

Elation! At least one church would give us a hearing!

" . . . but Presbyterians are prolific vacationers, so it might be a while before we decide," he added.

The following morning I copied our paperwork and made a personal appearance. Their tall, strapping pastor chatted with me for thirty precious minutes but, to my dismay, on another topic. I left with a heavy heart, certain he had second thoughts and planned to discard the papers.

◄o►

Our family's trip to conference in Seattle was approaching rapidly, so time was of essence now. Shortly before we left, I found myself gazing absent-mindedly into the bathroom mirror, my image hazy and blurred. What if the Presbyterians didn't follow through? Even if their pastor encourages sponsorship, what if his congregation says "no"? A negative response would crush me. I seriously doubted that my resilience was strong enough to navigate me to the phone again.

Almost afraid to hope, I dialed another number . . . the Ashland Brethren near Bryan.

Reaction # 6: "I don't know what our people will think, but we have a council meeting on Tuesday. I'll bring up the possibility."

Tuesday? I thought. *But we'll be out of town by then.*

I scampered to the typewriter, pounded a letter and delivered it with a fist full of papers. I added Billie and Earl's phone number in the event they had questions while Herb and I were gone.

—◦—

At last, the day came to leave. Herb and the children were excited. I was, too, except for the fact that I left my heart back in Bryan.

We headed West on Rt. 90 towards the Great Plains and Rocky Mountains. Camping in the Black Hills, Sioux Falls, Yellowstone, and Yosemite, we had a wonderful reprieve together as a family.

Adam, our budding scientist, enhanced his rock collection at various sites. MiRan cupped her nose and complained when sulfur emitted its gas from the geysers at Dragon's Mouth and the Sulfur Caldrons.

Nineteen hundred miles and ten days later, we rolled into Seattle. Herring gulls glided in narrowing circles—"keeah-keeah, kau-kau"—evidence we were nearing the Pacific. Reaching skyward in its elegant grandeur, the Space Needle's steely glass pinnacle reflected the glittering sunlight.

—◦—

A few hours later, amidst a crowd of 5,000 on the conference floor, we caught a glimpse of home. There they were . . . Paul and Betty with Florence and Kedric, soaking up the displays. Unlike the calm of moments before, arms tangled and laughter lilted through the arena as we greeted each other.

The natural flush in Paul's cheeks gave way to a boyish grin. "When did you folks arrive?" He beamed. A bit more shy than her husband, Betty's eyes danced happily as we chatted.

Herb said, "In this arena with thousands of people, it's amazing you and Betty are the first people we saw!" Then, answering Paul's question, he added, "We arrived Sunday night and camped in a gorgeous state park . . . "

" . . . under the airport!" I bellowed.

We laughed, recalling the silence of the night disrupted by roaring 747s landing at 5:00 a.m. The lush rain forest surrounding our tent seemed anachronistic to the noise of a twentieth century airport.

"That was our airplane!" Paul laughed. "We flew all night and got in early this morning."

Betty switched the subject. "Did you hear the news? The First Brethren Church in Bryan is sponsoring a family from Vietnam!"

I felt a low giggle escape from my throat. It bubbled up, and then, bellowed out in a shout of acclamation. The startled look on Paul's face told him we hadn't heard.

Apparently, the church's council asked Billie and Earl to present the need during worship the Sunday after we left, and their congregation voted an overwhelming affirmative. They, too, were going to resettle refugees.

A moment of jubilation!

An hour later, we discovered Myrna at the registration table processing new arrivals. Her line was long, so we shuffled closer in an adjacent one.

"Myrna," I whispered . . . "Hello!"

Her head snapped up. "Hi!" she said, her eyes shifting from us to new registrants awaiting their turn. As the first one left and the next one moved up, she said, "Have you heard? The Presbyterians are bringing a family to Bryan!"

"Myrna," I gasped. "You're kidding?"

"I'm not," she continued. "I spoke with June Webster, and she said . . ."

I never heard the rest of her statement. The clock struck 4:00 Pacific Standard Time in the arena, and everyone in the convention center at that particular moment could plainly see that I was busy soaring up to the seventh Heaven and back.

17
Firehole of Power

Yellowstone

Conference energized us, as did the vacation that followed. From Seattle, we wound our way east across the asphalt ribbon of highway, through the Columbia Plateau, and into the Rocky Mountains. After a night sleeping in sagebrush under the stars at Lewis and Clark, we began the uphill trek through spectacular Earthquake Valley, better known as The Yellowstone. The blue, sunny days wore well with our souls.

We watched, transfixed, as boiling cauldrons spewed black ash along-side jutting mountains. Pitted paint-pots poured labyrinths of color into the Firehole River in 20-foot sheets of rising steam. We sniffed the sulphur geysers, allowing their wind-blown spray to refresh our sweaty faces.

A small white sign pointed into the trees, indicating that something lay beyond us. Curiosity enticed us to follow the path to the Yellowstone's Upper Falls.[13]

This was no ordinary waterfall. Had we seen it from any other angle, it certainly might have been, but we stood above those falls, indeed, only a few feet from where millions of tons of water made the bend that dropped it, crashing, more than a hundred feet down to the rocks below.

Examining its trajectory upstream, the Yellowstone flowed and rippled lazily much like any tributary, but just beyond us, before it reached the larger falls, a sudden drop created a crashing power that changed the character of that river. Once its waves hit the turning point, it curved over the ledge, committing itself to dropping the remainder of the distance.

At that moment, the waters churned, their lazy ripples crashing to a thunderous roar—whitecaps twisting, gushing, annihilating, re-creating Chaos!

---

[13] For a movie of Yellowstone's Lower Falls, see www.yellowstonepark.com/2014/01/3
-waterfalls-of-the-grand-canyon-of-yellowstone. Scroll down toward the bottom of the
website to view it.

I stood transfixed, its spray soaking my being. The water seemed to scream at me, but it was not a scream of terror. Amidst the deafening roar a voice seemed to whisper my name . . .

"Join me, Jeanne. Examine the origins of my Power!"

My soul began to yearn for the secrets of that River. The Power! Oh, the Power!

Fixing my eyes on the pinnacle, I focused on its origin and followed the falls' trajectory. We crashed; we tossed; we roared, moving swiftly toward the crest—churning, turning, bursting all the schema for falls I'd ever seen before. My stomach floated to the top of my head, and with a mighty roar millions of gallons gushed with me, churning, turning, crashing into thousands of slivers of icy glass, soon to be swallowed by the cascade swelling toward the gorge.

Oh, the Power—the frightening, awe-inspiring Power!

Transfixed by the crashing falls dashing the boulders below, I saw them hit with such thunderous force that they spewed their gushing foam into millions of droplets, rising with such fury and might that it anointed my soul with fire.

Oh, the Power of that mighty Fall!

My mind reeled with mixed emotions. If Nature in all God's majesty, created these simple falls from raindrops and nothing more, if we could but reach out and touch them, perhaps we could cause a whirlwind of Power unlike anything we'd seen before.

Oh, the Power—that All-Encompassing Power!

I turned aside, my mind swirling with prayer.

―◄○►―

Frightened by the thunderous roar, MiRan grasped Herb's hand and held on tightly as we descended. Adam, our little scientist, continued his specimen hunting.

"Hey, Mom," he whispered, approaching a furry creature. "See the chipmunk over there?"

Adam inched his way toward it gingerly, holding out a cracker. Accustomed to human offerings, the ball of fur drew near, and then backed up, doubtful of the donor's intentions. A minute later, the little fellow tried again and this time was rewarded.

A gentle breeze sang through the giant timbers. And then, as though sharing an intimate secret with the falls, the thought flooded my soul: "Jeanne . . . you can grasp that Power if only you will claim it!"

My head lowered, but for the beauty of the moment, I dared not close my eyes. 'O God,' I cried, 'give me the courage to not relent, to grasp Your power, to follow!

Daunted at what I dared ask of the Almighty, I mouthed the remaining words carefully: "God, carry me with You over these falls to do what we need to do."

Awed by the beauty, we turned to leave the trees, the chipmunks, the River. None knew that I flowed with that River over the falls. None heard The Power's calling except for me. I breathed the deep earthy air and filled my lungs to bursting.

"Amen," I whispered. "Amen!"

18
Malaysian Nightmare

Escape!

Conference was encouraging. Back in Ohio, we tackled anew the church's mission with vigor. The day we arrived, Herb went to the office, leaving me with the children. I smiled at MiRan's and Adam's boisterous shenanigans as they scrambled at the sound of the doorbell.

Bi's face lit up when she saw me. "Chean, you're home!"

Her arms reached out to hug me.

She stooped down to MiRan, smiling broadly. Then, she grasped her chubby arms and said, "Mi-wan, how are you today?"

MiRan squeaked a trite "OK," then scampered outside to play with My. Adam's toothy grin flaunted giddy pleasure as he galloped around the carpet with Tuan astride his back. A few minutes later, they tangled in a lopsided wrestling match, with Adam mocking groans of misery as Tuan pinned his legs to the floor.

"I weed your gar-den, Chean," Bi said. "Wilma help me!"

"I heard you did," I chuckled. "She told me at conference that you wouldn't stop working until it rained!"

We rehashed the weeks we spent apart. Bryan's Fourth-of-July celebration had horrified the family. Sitting in Trudy's backyard, they ran inside for cover. Wailing rockets speeding in air, followed by earth-shaking blasts brought back the memories of war. My and Tuan screamed through it all, as brilliant displays shot into the darkness.

Beauty for one can spell misery for another.

◄○►

Back in May, Hanh hoed the soil in front of their apartment to plant a small garden. Now they were reaping its bounty.

When I arrived at their complex the next morning, Bi was busy dunking tomatoes into boiling water. She seemed quite comfortable with the process. In a matter of minutes, she lifted their carcasses from the kettle, pulled the hulls from the fruits, and slid them into scalded jars. I decided to stay and help her.

"Bi," I asked, "What was your home like in Vietnam."

Her eyes grew large as she began her saga. "We lif' near big water, Chean."

"You mean close to the sea?"

"No," she corrected, "a river. Water go close Hanh's father house. In morning, water go this way," . . . her finger sketched a rivulet flowing in one direction, "and at night water go other way." Her hand re-traced the inlet flowing backwards.

I cocked my head sideways, confused.

"But, Bi," I asked, "how can water go this way sometimes, and then, go the other? That's impossible."

"It can!" she enunciated. Then, countering my skepticism, she added, "I don' know why, but it do. Hanh go water many times. He throw big 'net', you say?"

"Yes, net."

"He throw big net in water. He get shremp."

"Shrimp?"

"Yes, shremp."

The pieces were falling together now.

"Did you live near the sea?"

Bi craned her neck in my direction. "What you say?"

"The sea!" I stretched my arms out in a circle. "The big water near the land."

Bi ignored my strange language lesson and continued.

"We lif' six month wit' Uncle."

"You did?"

She pinched the gold band on her finger. "Uncle haf' this . . . he haf' money. When Nor' Vietnam come, he hide money in garden."

I looked at Bi's wide eyes. She was learning to trust now. Her efforts would be rewarded if only I would listen.

In the background, the jars rattled fitfully as gas hissed the canner to a bubbly boil. We had forty five minutes without interruption until the batch would be finished.

Bi began to talk, her eyes downcast. "Chean, when Uncle pay for our family go boat, we hide on little . . . " she fumbled, searching for the precise word . . . "little land. We go on boat to . . . " she puzzled again.

I proffered, "a little 'island'?"

"Yes, little i'land. We hide many days in house, down very dark."

A cellar, I surmised.

"Eighty-one people, everybody hide. Little baby, t'ree month old, we give medicine. It sleep, sleep all the time. If baby one year, we give medicine . . . they don' talk, don' cry. But baby four month to one year, we cannot give. Baby sometimes cry."

Bi's troubled eyes fell quickly to the table, her fingers twitching in her hands. She swallowed hard and peered out the window as if talking to herself. "Uncle say we cannot keep Ngoc My. She six mon' old. She maybe cry. He take my baby back to Hanh's mother, father."

I sensed what happened, but remained silent.

An eclipse of darkness shaded Bi's eyes as she stumbled through an ominous explanation. "Soldiers come to house where we hide. We mus' be veddy quiet," she said. "My friend's baby, she cry. A man come to baby . . . "

She clenched her hands in choking fashion to her neck, as if re-living a terrifying moment. "He afraid. He do this."

The anxiety written on her face told me he wanted to suffocate it.

It hurt to hear Bi talk like that. I didn't want to hear more. Feeling miserably tactless, I pushed back my chair and suggested we take time for tea.

"No," she whispered. 'Si' down. Chean!'

Bi was a survivor and she needed someone to listen.

Suddenly, I realized that Bi was not the awkward one. Rather, it was I. She had a compulsion to tell her story, and I, a citizen of the affluent West, unconcerned with the heartache of hers, would have to restrain myself and listen.

"Chean, sit down!" she said again. The mother, father of baby I tell you, they stuff cloth in baby's mouth. Baby die."

Throwing her head back, tears streaked her cheeks. "I glad Ngoc My wit' Uncle now."

I sat silent, listening.

Bi's blue-black waves shifted from one shoulder to the other. Turning her head in my direction, a stream of information gushed fourth. Finally, she had an audience.

"On boat, five night, four day, Chean. We down, down in hold. Can not see sun. Little food." Her pinched fingers measured their meager rations. "I cry for Ngoc My and cannot eat. I gif' my food, My 'n' Tuan. Ef'rybody hungry."

I observed Bi closely, my mind recording every detail of her expression.

The palm of her hand curved slow, starving circles around her stomach, as her mouth spread wide to show their gnawing hunger.

"What about the captain and the crew? Did they have food?"

"Two men," she corrected, holding up two fingers, "they drive boat. They eat."

She changed the topic then.

"Smell . . . veddy bad on boat."

I paused and measured my words, trying to be sensitive. "So, what did you do for a restroom, Bi?"

She responded honestly, curling an imaginary drape across her slender body. "We put blanket 'round us . . . like this. Tha's all."

"Then we go Malaysia," she added.

"I tell you how we go Malaysia, come Ame'dica, Chean?" she asked in a lighter inflection.

I grasped the opportunity to fetch a pitcher of sun tea. Turning my face from her steady gaze, hot tears welled in back of my eyes as I fumbled awkwardly with the glasses.

Was this my friend? In the few months since Bi's arrival, the walls of culture, race, religion, and language that stood between us came crumbling down, dissolving our differences into a common bond of compassion and understanding.

A cool whoosh of air gushed across my face as the refrigerator door slid shut. The children heard the muffled plump of rubber on enamel and scurried to the kitchen.

I filled four empty glasses, then poured refills and dumped the ice cubes in the sink. Draining the last of the brew into Bi's glass, I hustled the children from the room, Peanuts' style, back into the playroom.

◄○►

"Bi, tell me about Malaysia."

I leaned into her answer.

"We in Malaysia nine months," she said. "Ef'ry day I cook."

"What did you cook?"

"They give us food. We don' like, but everybody take. No gar'ten."

"Where were you in Malaysia, Bi?"

"Don' know."

"Adam, bring me your globe!" I called.

His head popped around the corner bearing the blue-green orb perched on a metal stand.

"Now, Bi, where in Malaysia?"

She fingered the Asian territories, as though looking for people, rice paddies, and maybe a few pigs and dogs, assuming they'd come into focus if she could stare hard enough.

Finally, she fixated her eyes on a tiny dot. Her index finger underlined the fine print: "Pulau Bidong."

My heart sank. We heard too much about Pulau Bidong. In Seattle at conference Herb and I had visited with Mac Coffman, the manager of refugee resettlement at Church World Service. Mac had returned from Pulau Bidong just weeks before.

"That was the most miserable place I've ever been," he told us somberly. "Disease, hunger, and TB run rampant. The people are desperate and extremely grateful for all we do for them.

"When our time was up," he continued, "our craft sailed away. Thousands waded out to sea after our boat in waist deep water with their arms outstretched, crying for us to take their plea to the people of America."

I recalled vividly the pain in Mac's eyes as he recounted his experience. "I get emotional every time I talk about what I saw there," he said. "Several times I told myself, 'Get hold of yourself, Mac. You'll do more good if you don't lose control.'"

◄○►

Clearly, Bi and Hanh were living evidence of Mac's experience. In the maelstrom of misery, war and oppression, their story mirrored thousands of others.

During the course of our conversation, Bi's arms swept out expansively. "We lif' big boat," she said. "Many people, no walls."

Apparently, each family nestled in its own enclave.

"Where did you keep your clothing, Bi?" I prodded.

She looked at me confused, then blushed and spoke. Laying her hands on her shirt, she said, "We wear what we haf."

"That's all?"

Her eyes fell, timidly. "Tha's all."

"Was it difficult?"

"Yeah," she said, somewhat lamely. "Not so good, take bath." She stood up and tapped our faucet, searching for the word.

"Spigot?" I offered.

Only one water . . . 'spigot', you say . . . for many people. We drink, we cook, wash hair, ef'rybody, same-same 'spigot.'"

Her eyes grew large, and I urged her on. Catharsis was in process.

"My family in Malaysia, long time. Our friends go Ame'dica, go France, go Canada. One day, 'man Ame'dica' come boat. Hanh talk to man. He say he come Wednesday to say who can go. Many nights Hanh cannot sleep. I cannot sleep."

Bi drifted into nervous laughter, then continued.

"On Wednesday man come like he say. He talk like this, like this," she said, holding an invisible megaphone to her face.

"Many people—t'ousand people—come hear man Ame'dica."

Bi shielded her eyes as if peering over a distant crowd. "Man talk, talk, talk. My 'n' Tuan tired. They cry. I say, 'Be quiet! Man talk'!"

Bi revved up the volume rapidly now, excited. "He say, 'Hanh, Bi, My an' Tuan, an' he talk, talk, talk!' I so happy, I clap, clap, clap! My 'n' Tuan go friends. They say, 'We cannot play wit' you anymore. We mus' go Ame'dica now!'

"Our friends, they happy, too!"

Sinking into her chair with a contented glow, the young mother's eyes danced with exuberance.

I shivered. Bi had just shared their story—how they were chosen for freedom. Suddenly, tears welled in my eyes. I pulled her to me and gave her a hug.

"Bi, we're so happy you're with us!"

All this time Bi's heartache had festered inside. Now that she could share their story, we could see them through another set of eyes.

19

Empathy—"For the Least of These"

Walking in Their Moccasins

Walking in Bi's *G`iay*[14]

A blanket of stillness lay over the night as the eerie darkness created wooing sounds. I could almost hear my heart beat.

The clock on our bureau resonated with a purring hum. MiRan's pillow shuffled in her room next door, as big brother Adam crinkled fresh sheets in his loft down the hall, followed by a faint snore. Herb shuffled his head from left to right when a car whisked by outside our window on the second floor.

We had so many experiences with Bi and Hanh that I felt compelled to record them. To that end, I found myself in a habitual state of sleeping with pen and notebook beneath my pillow. On nights when the moon didn't shine, my left thumb positioned itself at the top left corner. As each thought came to fruition, I slipped my thumb down a notch to begin a new line. The system worked reasonably well if I refrained from dotting '*i*'s and crossing '*t*'s.

Mornings often found me deciphering sentences, one overlaid on the other. But if the aesthetics proved problematic, in daylight, at least, the basics were there for unraveling. I loved those late night rendezvous with my Muse.

Partway into my musings that night, Herb tossed and drowsily rolled over.

"Jeanne," he groaned, "must you write with that noisy pen?" And with that, he lulled back to sleep.

I hadn't thought about my pen being noisy.

---

14 Vietnamese is a tonal language. Depending on the tone with which a word is spoken, its meaning can change. 'G`iay', for example, refers to a 'shoe' when spoken in a tone resembling the end of a sentence. This must be differentiated between 'G`iay' with a falling tone, meaning 'question', and 'G`iay' spoken without fluctuation, which refers to 'a second'. (*Languages in the World: How History, Culture, Politics, Shape Language*. Julie Tetel Andresen, 2015).

109

Though my body ached with weariness, insomnia reigned, my mind darting wildly from one thought to another.

The moon wisped a beam of light into our room, barely enough to decipher the notebook by my pillow. Groping for a pen, the words began to flow. Little did I know the catharsis I would wrestle with that night.

I began . . .

"You, Jeanne, have been blessed with twenty-seven years of life on this Earth. Herb has graced it for twenty-eight."

I thought about Herb and myself at Hanh and Bi's ages in our twenties. By then, we both had earned bachelor's degrees. After our wedding, we took off for Chicago in our '62 Studebaker so Herb could finish seminary. Two years later, we moved to Virginia where I earned my master's in English. In time, we criss-crossed the country to Claremont, California, where our son, Adam, was born as Herb completed his doctorate. A few years later, we adopted our little daughter MiRan, our 'beautiful orchid' from Korea.

Though we had our struggles, we were blessed.

◄o►

From midnight until 3:00 a.m., I pieced together everything we knew about them—Hanh's thrashing by the soldiers, Uncle's compassion, his aunt's anger, their decision to flee, their time in hiding, the pirates, the storms at sea, landing in Malaysia and, finally, their struggle to shore in the thrashing waves where they mercifully found asylum.

In short, more than most of us could bear.

That night, I re-lived every heartbreaking event that they shared with us. Through tears, I wrote and wept and, when weary, I prayed.

Writing frantically, I fought back tears at every juncture of their journey. Nothing could erase their tortured heartache from my soul.

At one point, I revolted. *Jeanne! Stop flagellating yourself this way!* But my troubled mind persisted. I yearned to heave my papers to the floor but the words kept pouring. I was sentenced to write their story to the finish. There would be no release until the power of the written word had freed me from their bondage.

◄o►

" . . . Dear Reader, walk with me now in Bi's moccasins. Slip inside her skin and search her soul. Re-live her family's struggle to find a country that they could call 'home'.

Children:

Bi – gave birth to four children, the two who fled with her and Hanh, a stillborn child, and a baby back home.

Jeanne – gave birth to one son and adopted a daughter from Korea.

Education:

Bi – Unknown

Jeanne – Bachelor's and Master's degrees from accredited universities.[15]

Home:

Bi can never go home again.

Jeanne returns home to visit her family once or twice each year."

Walking in Her G`*iay*[16]

"Bi of Vietnam" juxtaposed with "Jeanne of the USA"

You, Bi, are 27 years old. Your husband is 26. You gave birth to four children in six years of marriage. Sadly, one was stillborn. Another is thousands of miles away, lost perhaps, forever.

You live in a land trampled by war and invaders. They hacked down your fruit trees, all 150 of them. The culprits rampaged your land, leaving you with no means of survival.

Your husband has been harboring resentment for some time. He's so upset that he does something unwise: he resists.

"Three years of oppression are enough," he says.

But his resistance has repercussions. Invaders break into your home one day and take your husband by force. They tie him to a chair with his hands behind his back, then kick and beat him so badly that his stomach is internally damaged.

His assailants release him after a week of barbaric treatment. He finds his way home, his spirit broken. Your family lives in constant fear that soldiers will attack again.

One day, Uncle confers with your husband. He tells him he's on the invaders' hit list. Your very lives are in jeopardy.

You must flee, but where? The territory to the North is at war with you. The country to your west is burdened with those who fled before you. If you cross the border now, you'll be shot or thrown into prison. Rumors are cir-

---

[15]The author earned her B.A. at Elizabethtown College, Elizabethtown, Pennsylvania (1966), followed by her M.A. at James Madison University (1969). In 1999, before the publication of this book, she received the Ed.D. from Kansas State University.

---

[16] 'G`iay': 'shoes' in Vietnamese. Our Native American equivalent: "Walking in her moccasins."

culating that others are buried alive. To the South and East is the sea. Where can you flee?

Uncle visits you under cover of night. He talks casually for a few minutes, then lowers his voice.

You hear him quietly mumbling. As the minutes slip by, his decibels grow louder, almost angry, convincing your husband he's in danger.

Husband nods his head.

Uncle shrinks back into the shadows and takes leave.

That evening in bed your husband shares something you don't want to hear. You're going to abscond, to leave your homeland. It will change the trajectory of your lives. You lay awake the rest of the night, worrying.

The next day you try to act casual, but your heart is pounding. What if Uncle's plans fall through? What if you are caught? You push fear back into the recesses of your mind and concentrate on survival.

That night, very late, with only the clothing on your back and the meager rations you can carry, you go into hiding. Before leaving, you bow to your parents, bid them farewell, and try to restrain your tears. When you go, you dare not look back. You are a married woman now, and you must obey your husband.

Your farm near the sea borders the Mekong on the Southern tip of the country. Your eyes grow accustomed to darkness as you run, then hide, and run again. At a designated place, you draw into the shadows and meet Uncle. His wife is angry. She has no desire to leave, but has no choice in the matter. He ignores her and leads you to a small vessel. You scramble on board with the children.

Uncle rows along the dark shoreline, dipping in along the way to hide in the dense foliage. Finally, he executes a sharp turn out to sea.

Minutes later, you approach a small, craggy island protruding up from the sea. Under cover of night, Uncle hides his vessel in the marshy waters and helps you disembark.

You grope nervously toward a bungalow shadowed in the moonlight. Pushing aside the brush, you cautiously enter the structure. Uncle and his wife follow.

Two silhouettes approach in the dark.

"You have come for the *thuyèn* [boat]?"

"*Có,*" you say. [Yes]

"*ông oó máy cháu*? [How many children?]"

"*Ba,*" you answer. [Three]

"*Đi theo tôi.*" [Follow us]

The strangers lead you down under the deck, into a dark hold. Occupied by silhouettes, several stir as you enter. Others, exhausted, are deep in sleep. The five of you collapse on the floor and spend a restless night together.

Before daybreak, a pang of fear stabs through you. Soldiers are outside! My and Tuan clam up with fear. The baby senses your tension, and she begins to cry. You crouch into a corner, huddling her tightly against your breast, but she continues her wailing.

The soldiers are advancing, closer. They're running now, and they have guns! You must not be caught, or all of you will die!

Their heavy footsteps come close, and then, their voices fade.

Exhausted, you breathe deeply. My and Tuan cling to your shirt, too terrified to cry. Even your husband is trembling. Both of you sense what must be done, but you don't have the courage to do it.

—◄○►—

That night, Uncle steals to your hiding place. He has food.

Husband tells him what happened.

Uncle looks grave, then makes the decision for you.

"We must take the baby back," he says. "Take her back to my brother, to her grandparents."

You recoil and open your mouth to speak, but you cannot find your voice.

Husband pleads with him—how much time before the boat to freedom comes? Can you keep the child until then?

Uncle's answer slices the silence. "The baby could disclose our hiding place at any given moment. We cannot control her cries. If we are caught, all of us will perish."

"Besides," he adds, "she could die on this journey." He heard many did on these illegal voyages out of the country.

Uncle promises she'll be brought to you when they learn that the boat is coming.

—◄○►—

Nights later a small craft pulls ashore. No one has come with Ngoc My yet, but you board, as instructed. You paddle out to sea under cover of night.

Uncle rows out to join you. His disgruntled wife accompanies him.

113

With anxiety, he whispers, "I am so sorry, but there was no time to retrieve her! I am so sorry!"

Aunt turns away from you, upset.

A lump forms in your throat. You swoon and almost faint.

Uncle reports that, with the exception of your mother-in-law, no one knows about your departure. Hanh's father thinks you're visiting Can Tho. Your parents know nothing about you leaving. If they did, they would be heartsick.

On board, My and Tuan cling to you for consolation. You draw them close and wonder if they'll ever see Ngoc My again. The palm of your hand massages your heavy breasts. You feel the soreness there and know she's nursed her last from you.

Confused, the children peer into your eyes. They don't understand the word, 'forever.'

You're not alone in your grief. Others on board left loved ones, too, but none had to abandon a tiny, six-month-old daughter.

Your husband is silent, solemnly so. Stoically, he weeps but refuses to show his emotions. He tries to comfort you, but what can he do? He is helpless, too.

—◦—

DAY 1 – At daybreak, your *thuyền đánh cá*[17] enters the South China Sea, sailing away from soldiers and invaders. Spoon-billed sandpipers break the silence with threats above your vessel. You cannot see the ocean because you are down in the hold. It is dark inside. Eighty-one people are sailing with you, too many for your small craft. Food and water are scarce, but you're too upset to eat anyway, so give your share to the children. There is no restroom. The deck smells rank.

DAY 2 – The old man dies. They bury him at sea. Two more follow in the evening hours.

DAY 3 – Your stomach rumbles. You feed your meager rations to the children. The captain and crew have all the food they want.

DAY 4 – You sight land in the distance. Two more fall ill today. Can they make it to shore for help?

3:00 p.m. – You enter territorial waters. Someone rows out to interrogate you. They are police. They demand that you leave. It's the jurisdiction's

---

[17] *thuyền đánh cá* – fishing boat

policy. Too many arrived in the days and nights before you. You push back to sea.

5:30 p.m. – You arrive at a second port, enduring another interrogation. Loud shouts ensue between captain and the officers. You begin to feel hopeless.

8:10 p.m. – Shortly before nightfall, captain sights an enclave. Turning leeward toward the palm-lined shore, your craft halts suddenly with a jarring thud. Treacherous shoals mar your stern, wrenching metal and shattering wood. Your boat is leaking now. Husband joins the brigade to dip, but water gushes across the deck faster than they can bail it. Captain conspires with his crew. What now to do? You stare numbly at them dipping . . . cursing . . . shouting.

Fear shatters all illusions. Your survival instinct sets in. You are determined to live for the sake of your children. You strap My to your husband's back, and he straps the smaller Tuan to yours. Many passengers are wailing. Others stay back to die. They cannot swim or are too old and weak to try. But you lived near water all your life, and the sea is your second nature.

With a deep breath, you lower yourselves down the side of the stern, the boat perilously close to capsizing.

Others slide down after you. Frightened, and gulping salt water, you dip long strokes in an easterly direction. Your muscles twist, fighting the waves. Tuan, on your back, is screaming, but your daughter, My, synchronizes her paddling with Husband's. You wish your load were as easy, but yours kicks and cries.

The shoreline, with each paddle, comes closer. They must accept you there! You swim, catching glimpses of Husband. My, on his back, no longer thinks it's a game and pokes her head high to swallow air. Tuan, on yours, howls when he isn't gulping, but you're glad he does. At least, you know he's alive.

Shore is only a few minutes yonder. You gasp for breath. As your arms glide from one side to the other, passengers frantically fight the waves and the undercurrent. This leg of the trip is hazardous.

Minutes later, your feet sink toward the ocean floor in your struggle with the sea. The tide retracts from the shoreline, as high as your chest, pushing hard, swallowing the waves. You fight to thrust yourself forward. You don't have energy to persevere, but you do.

Men on the shore wade out to rescue you. Two grasp you under your shoulders, and you collapse in their arms. They untie My from Hanh's back. A kindly matron comes running to quell her shivering body. You would, but your eyes blur into purple, and then to red, and finally into blackness. As brutally as it began, the ordeal fades into oblivion.

─◄o►─

Some time later, you awaken. Husband sits at your side, staring. You don't know it yet, but the creases around his eyes have forever destroyed the boy in him, leaving only a man to fight the demons.

My and Tuan sleep soundly now. Later that night, she cries out in a nightmare, a common occurrence in these camps. Your husband lies awake, moving restlessly by your side. He wonders if it's been worth it . . . estranged from his country without a home, belonging to no one, lost at sea, and no-body cares.

But he knows something you don't know: Of the 80 on board your boat, only ten survived.

Your family was among them.

─◄o►─

Each night in camp, you sleep side by side with others. Days are spent rummaging for firewood onshore to cook your meager rations. Nutrition leaves much to be desired.

You learn you are pregnant again. In the seventh month of gestation, your baby is stillborn. You were hoping it would be a girl to divert your atten-tion from Ngoc My who was left behind.

You live side-by-side with others on the island for eight months. You're used to working, earning your keep, but to survive you must learn to receive. This is not your manner of living.

─◄o►─

Finally, the day arrives. After months in camp, your day has come for an interview. You wash your clothes in the sea and lay them on rocks to dry. You must make a good impression. There is no second chance.

Your number is finally called. An American interviews you through an interpreter. He is much taller than other men you know, and heavy. No one in Vietnam is obese. He speaks strange words through an interpreter, who passes them on to you.

Your husband answers obediently, so nervous he scarcely recalls what was said, except that on Wednesday the man will return. Then he will say who has been chosen and who has not. You suffer sleepless nights until then.

─◄o►─

At high noon, you and hundreds of others trace your steps to the compound. The crowd stretches as far as one can see. The man speaks into a megaphone, calling out names of those who can leave.

You listen and you listen. Your children become impatient. You silence them so you can hear. Many, many names are called. Finally, you weary of listening but, then, you hear: 'Nguyen Huu Hanh, Tran Tri Bi, Nguyen Kim My, Nguyen Anh Tuan'. . .and The Voice drones on.

—◄○►—

For the first time in months, you belt out a hearty laugh. Your friends are happy for you. Your husband is brave and hides his emotions, but both of you are relieved.

My bounds around telling her friends, "We cannot play wit' you anymore. We must go Ame'dica now!"

Little Tuan is confused. He studies your face and knows that something good is happening to his family.

That night you and your husband laugh and cry in each other's arms, for someone in the world out there, people you've never seen, whose names you can't even pronounce, are reaching out to tell you, "We care. Come live with us. We'll help you regain your dignity. We'll find you a home and a job. And with God's help, maybe—just maybe—we'll find your baby, too."

—◄○►—

Exhausted from walking through Bi's heartache, I dried my tears. No wonder the family was grateful. They had braved the odds of fate and survived. And now, we as a church entrusted with their healing had the awesome responsibility of gathering up the fragments of their lives and piecing them back together again.

Like a starved child whose hunger escapes in the welcome amnesia of sleep, I collapsed into a deep slumber.

The Nguyens were strangers no more.

20
News from Home

Their letters penetrate Vietnam.

Over the weeks my lively sense of the ridiculous became engaged, and I played mental gymnastics with infiltration into Vietnam to retrieve the Nguyen baby. But quixotic fantasies come and go, and reality came full circle.

I shuddered at the trust Hanh and Bi invested in us. We promised them we would explore every available option to reunite their family, and they had a childlike faith that we would follow through. Thus, we wrote letters and made phone calls to our legislators, the State Department, Immigration Service, Church World Service, and others.

The family knew our extra measures were beyond the call of duty.

━◄○►━

Each day, my patience grew shorter. "Herb," I said one evening, "I'm calling Senator Glenn tomorrow to see if he's making progress." The words came out more like a mandate than a statement.

Herb dropped *The Sporting News* in his lap. He glanced at me staring at him and missed the concern in my eyes.

"Long distance?"

"Yes."

"Then, write another letter," he drawled, immersing himself back in his article.

"But, Herb," I persisted," It's been three weeks! The legislature adjourned last Friday. He could be leaving the country for all we know!"

His mouth gapped open as if to protest, but then, he changed his mind. "It's important to you, isn't it?"

I darted a furtive glance in his direction. "Yes, my dear. This is extremely important!"

He stared at me for an elongated moment.

"Then do what you must do."

—◄o►—

An aide answered, a very efficient one. He showed more than diplomatic interest in the Nguyens' case and promised to return the call after learning the whereabouts of our letter.

For three days I chained myself to the house waiting for the phone to ring. When the call finally came, I clung tenaciously to the receiver, listening intently.

Genuine concern filtered through the aide's sandy voice. "Your letter, Ms. Smith, is in the Department of Health, Education and Welfare. It's being forwarded from Washington and will be in our office shortly."

"In other words, you haven't read it yet?"

"No," he added, "but I'll be with you as soon as we have time to do the research."

—◄o►—

Twelve days later, we received the letter. It was not heartening.

I stared out the window, past the fields and trees surrounding our parsonage. *I'm running out of ideas,* I thought.

"And time," Fate added, silently.

The puzzle of retrieving Hanh and Bi's baby found pieces here and there throughout the world and helter-skelter in the states. But one lone piece remained abandoned, lost, detached from the umbilical cord of its existence, at least for the time being.

We didn't have the heart to tell Hanh and Bi for several weeks.

—◄o►—

I eased our car along the driveway, drifting to a halt in front of their apartment. My and Tuan heard the engine and came chattering out to meet us. When I finally shut down the motor, they scampered to open the door on the passenger side.

Adam stretched across the seat and pulled the latch inside. The door sprang open.

My and Tuan flew backwards, but the sudden startle did not keep them from chattering. Their happy cries tumbled over each other in their haste to tell all at once.

Adam and MiRan joined the chorus, and by the time we reached their apartment, we knew something special had happened.

Bi sprang to the door to greet us. "Chean," she cried, a huge smile glowering on her countenance. She hugged me quickly, then pushed me back and shouted, "Today we get letter from Uncle in Calnifornya! He get letter from Daddy, Mommy, Vietnam!"

"Bi, I gasped, "are they all right?"

"Yeah," she said, beaming. "They OK!"

Stepping inside, Hanh nodded his head to greet us, then deposited himself on the sofa.

"Here, Chean, I show you," he said.

Whisking the letter from the envelope, he unfolded it in his lap. A half page of hieroglyphs sang out as he interpreted the message.

"Uncle say my mother, my father, goot. They in Vietnam and happy we in Ame'dica!"

He looked toward me, seeking a pleasurable reaction.

This was good news, indeed very good news! And, yes, I was happy for them. They had waited for this moment much too long.

I grinned and asked, "Are you happy that Uncle wrote?"

"Yes!" they beamed together. "Veddy happy! Veddy, veddy happy."

". . . because," Bi continued, "our parents don' know if we die in sea. Now . . . " Her hands grasped the letter and she held it high as though she had won a marathon. " . . . they know!"

Hanh's brow crinkled, revealing his anxiety. "Chean, many people leave my country; they die. Mommy, daddy, don' get our letters. They t'ink we die, too. But now . . ."

As he spoke, the pathos that played in the corners of Hanh's eyes spoke for him. His parents were still in Vietnam, and they were alive. But they would, likely, never see each other again.

I cleared my throat, stalling for time, then tread thin ice with a question. "Does their letter say anything about your baby?"

A sudden sadness washed over them.

Hanh straightened in his seat, his eyes downcast. Bi's lids fluttered heavily over her prominent cheeks, her blood beating heavily in her throat.

Hanh spoke quietly. "No . . . not'ing about baby."

He lifted the letter up again, scanning its pages in vain for her name, which he knew did not exist there.

I tried to convince them that she was fine, that they had worked through this before, but nothing could assuage their emotions except concrete evidence from one who had seen her, firsthand.

"She was with your parents, wasn't she?"

"Yeah," Hanh's eyes told me. "I t'ink she wit' my parents now."

I dredged up a phony smile. "The letter says Hanh's family is all right. So your baby is all right, too." They accepted my words hungrily, wanting desperately to believe, but not quite daring to do so.

◄○►

"Daddy, why church people so good to us?" Hanh asked Earl after work one night. The young couple often wondered why strangers halfway around the world would care so much about helping them.

Earl draped his arm across Hanh's shoulder and tried earnestly to explain the common bond of humanity that tied us together as brothers and sisters. But the simplest explanation reduced to the lowest common denominator always emerged . . . "We love you, Hanh, because our God tells us to love you."

◄○►

Herb often teased Billie and Earl about giving our church a 'Cadillac' in lieu of a 'Volkswagen' when it came to hosting our family.

"Well, how else could we do it?" Billie asked, rather perturbed at the question.

Her answer gave rise to theological questions about our God. Billie and Earl, at various junctures, talked with Bi and Hanh about their faith, but the discussion inevitably led to their ancestry, a sacred subject in their world view.

At times we wished they could leave the past behind and forget the painful memories that severed their family ties. In America, they had a home, a job, freedom from fear, an adopted family, and a support group in the church. It would be so much easier to bury the past and begin anew.

Yet how could they possibly erase their identity, the last twenty-seven years of their lives? Roots run deeper than that. Roses do not yield daisies; they bear roses. Nor could either flower be severed from the stalk and hope to remain alive.

◄○►

Hanh's voice inflected as he tried to explain the ingrained tenants of their heritage. "Family is veddy important," he said. "My family haf' trouble, I mus' help."

Earl cast an appreciative eye toward him. "But how can you help them, Hanh, when they're in Vietnam and you are here?"

Hanh felt somewhat deflated by the scruples of Daddy America.

"Daddy, I can not go now, but if I lif' Vietnam, I mus' go my father house."

Hanh blinked his soft eyes behind the dark-rimmed glasses, newly purchased for his driver's exam. "I haf' cousin, lif' Saigon. His father die. He sell house, Saigon 'n' move to father house. He take care his mother."

Earl sought to make sense of an authoritative culture that demanded so much of its younger generation.

"You mean he gave up his job and everything?"

Hanh framed his face with his hands, then looked at the floor and nodded, "Yeah, in Vietnam, he mus' do."

◄O►

Chilly September mornings gave way to sunny afternoons. As Wilma loomed over The Book with Hanh and Bi one day, she exclaimed, "I don't mind teaching them English, but not this driving stuff!"

With winter weather threatening, our English teachers decided to take time out from Laubach and work with Hanh on the driver's manual. Shortly afterwards, Wilma and Florence staged a war against it, relinquishing the job to someone else.

Wondering what the problem was, Billie and I decided to peruse the manual.

"Look at this list!" Billie said as she flipped through the pages. "It's loaded . . . "

". . . with car parts!" I exclaimed. "Axis, chassis, gear shift, carburetor. No wonder they're discouraged!"

Billie slid back in her easy chair, exasperated. "Wilma and Mabel would need a class in mechanics to explain this stuff!"

I jammed my hands in my pockets and slid in the chair adjacent to hers. "Why do they have to know the names of all the car parts to drive it? I don't, and I've been driving for years!"

Bi's head riveted from one of us to the other, catching tidbits of the conversation.

"We need a translator," Billie stated flatly. "That's what we need."

"What about Chung?" I asked.

"No." She sulked. "He's studying to pass the language exam for veterinary medicine."

"Who else could help?"

Billie fooled with her coffee cup, thinking. "Maybe Mr. Tri could help us . . . the Vietnamese man in Defiance."

"Or what about Hon and Ming?" I asked.

Let's try Mr. Tri first," she said.

Bi broke in. "Chean, Thursday we go Defiance . . . Hanh teeth!"

"She's right, Billie. We can see him after Hanh's appointment."

"Don't plan on visiting then," she warned. "Hanh will be sick after his surgery. What about the following week when we return to remove his stitches?"

"Let's do it then," I said, relieved. "I'll drive."

—◦—

The specialist studied the X-rays by Hanh's side. Then, he peered intently down Hanh's throat. "Four molars are badly deteriorated," he reported.

I stood next to Hanh in the dentist's office, explaining the surgical jargon to him as best as I could. Minutes later, black spots danced before his eyes, and Hanh swam into oblivion under anesthesia. After the procedure was underway, I joined Bi who was busy watching the children out in the waiting room.

Nearly an hour passed before the nurse stepped through the door. "He's finished," she said, somewhat empathetically. "You may drive your car to the ramp in the rear of the building."

Red flags flew up as I met Bi's gaze. "I'll bet we have a sick man on our hands!"

"What you say?" she asked.

"Hanh is sick," I repeated.

My hunch proved correct. The nurse pivoted Hanh through the door in a large chrome wheelchair. An 'I-don't-care-about-anything' expression flushed illusively over his washed-out complexion. His mouth hung partially agape with cotton swabs stuffed in his jaws, and his head sat on his shoulders only because it was attached. I fully expected it to flop down on the pavement.

Sizing up our two-door Dodge, the back seat appeared more comfortable, but it would be a tight fit boosting him up and in. I pushed the driver's seat as close to the steering wheel as possible, while pondering how on earth we could lift him.

Moments later, I made a sudden turn-about, only to find Hanh wearily dragging himself out of the wheelchair, upright on his feet. He tottered and groped instinctively for the door handle.

Good, I thought. *Looks like he can get in himself!*

He lifted his foot up to the floor, and just as we expected him to position himself upright inside, he swung his weight forcefully around on his heel, and flopped across the entire length of the seat, his body parts sinking languidly wherever they happened to fall. Bi scooted his legs together and scrunched herself in beside him.

The kindly nurse startled, then asked, "She's going to sit back with him?"

"Guess so," I mumbled.

I locked the seat belt over his body, buckled MiRan in front with me, and breathed a sigh of relief that Billie had the rest of the kids at home.

A half hour later, we supported Hanh's arms as he staggered wobbly-kneed across the sidewalk. Inside he flopped lifelessly onto the sofa, dozing in and out of his torpor.

I left Bi alone, repeating the doctor's orders one more time.

"Next Tuesday, Bi, they'll take the stitches out."

◄○►

The following week, we repeated the trek. Hanh disappeared, as scheduled, into the dentist's office. A few minutes later, he traipsed behind a stern looking nurse who trotted briskly into the waiting room. Her demeanor reminded me of a frustrated teacher leading a disobedient child to the principal's office.

"He took them out himself!" she growled.

Hanh stood sheepishly at my side, wondering what punishment she might impose.

I shrugged my shoulders. "Then there's nothing else to do?"

She imped her face and sniffed. "No. You might as well go home!"

"Good!" I said, trying to hide my chuckles. "Let's go, Hanh!"

His look of surprise told me he expected more than that. I waited for the door to click before the grin sneaked across my face.

"Hanh, you did it yourself?" My shoulders quivered with a snicker that rose from deep inside.

"Yeah," he admitted, feeling somewhat foolish. Then, the impish boy lurking in the man broke into a grin, and together we belted out a great and lusty laugh.

◄○►

Hanh did not recognize street names or house numbers, but he led me directly to Mr. Tri's abode. His wife, Trang, greeted us warmly.

Their apartment's warm shag carpet and billowy furnishings were chosen with a lively eye for color. Oriental screens graced the southern wall. While an orange curtain fluttered out the window, petite dolls with almond eyes modeled their silken finery in shiny doll domes.[18]

Tri and Trang's family had lived in Defiance for four years, and their resettlement seemed complete. A local church helped us connect with them.

"Mr. Tri," I began, "we need someone to teach Hanh to drive."

"I can do?" he said.

"That would help tremendously," I said. "It's hard for us because we don't know Vietnamese."

I found myself wanting to transfer Hanh's language deficit to Tri unconsciously, but he and his wife knew English well, so our fears were unfounded.

"Can you translate the driver's manual for Hanh?"

They paused a moment. "I study driver book, too," Trang said. Her silky black hair bounced as she nodded her head in the affirmative. "I t'ink I can do."

Several weeks later, Trang and a friend returned the manual with diacritical markings of Vietnamese in every margin. We were extremely grateful and thanked her profusely for her help.

◄○►

I whiffed a sprig of dill and tucked it into the jar. Over the past year, I had developed a strange addiction to kosher dill pickles. I chuckled to myself, recalling how Bi and Hanh rumpled their noses when I offered them a bite.

Suddenly, the phone clattered, and my head shot up from the jars. Cradling the handset against my shoulder, I bit my lip, absorbing Bi's startling words. The blood drained from my face, as I backed into a kitchen chair, trembling. Losing all capacity to be objective, tears began to trickle.

Bi was ecstatic. "Today," she blurted, one word tumbling over the other, "I get two letter, Chean! One from sister, one from brother, Vietnam! Two letter from my family, Chean! They say Ngoc My . . . she walk, walk, walk! She talk, talk, talk! She say 'Mommy,' she say 'Daddy.' I so happy! I so happy!" Bi beamed her elation across the wires with a rush of joy.

"Bi! I'm happy for you!" I cried. "Call Hanh at work and tell him!"

She hung up, and a swell of warmth rushed through my chest, turning

---

18 Doll domes are glass showcases for vintage or ethnic dolls. Many have special significance to a culture. They are rarely used as toys for children.

into a shiver. Numbly, I placed the phone on its receiver, then turned to find Herb watching me.

"What's wrong, Jeanne? What did she say?"

My mouth fell open, but the words wouldn't come. Herb sensed the intensity of the moment, and his large arms swallowed me.

"It's about the baby, isn't it?"

I smiled vaguely and opened my mouth to speak, but my throat was coarse.

He pulled me close and laughed. "You silly woman! You're supposed to be laughing, not crying!"

"I am laughing," I wailed as I tossed back my head, my cheeks streaked with tears.

He cradled my face in his large hands and looked directly into my eyes. "You look like you're laughing, Jeanne. You're having a great time, aren't you?"

I dried my face on his shirt and pulled him fiercely to me. "Herb, there's something I must tell you."

Then, slowly, each syllable forced its way through my quivering lips, "This battle we have won, Herb! This one we have won!"

◄○►

One year and twenty seven days. Bi had not known in all that time the well-being of their infant.

Billie had told her she must pray, like "this", with her hands folded, for the sleepless nights and claw of constant worry tallied ill effects on Bi's physique, not to mention the anguish that ravaged her heart and soul.

On many occasions, Bi rolled her eyes toward Mommy America and said, "I do pray, Mommy, e'fry night. E'fry night I pray for Ngoc My."

During her spiritual struggle with fate, Bi somehow reached an invisible plateau. At that point, she stopped running from the pain she could no longer bear and turned to face it. But she didn't face the specter alone. She bore it with her God.

We did not know what god she bargained with, but somewhere in the Universe, her god reflected her understanding of the great God who loves us all. So she prayed, and reaching across the terrible darkness, we prayed with her.

21
The Inevitable Incident

The belching anger was out of proportion to the wound.

The next day we took a jaunt to their apartment. Seconds after turning off the ignition, Adam and MiRan, just home from school, took off for the swings with My and Tuan.

"What did their letters say," Bi?" I asked, as I settled into the sofa.

Her eyes burst into life. I didn't have to ask her twice.

"My Mommy, my Daddy," she said, "I so happy they write!"

Crossing the room to the kitchen cabinets, she located the letters on the counter top. Moments later, she sauntered back across the carpet, producing two envelopes bearing a strange language with militaristic stamps on the corner.

Hanh looked at them and sneered. "Nor' Vietnam defeat Saigon. That what stamp say!"

He pointed his finger accusingly at the triumphant tanks that shouted victory. They reminded him bitterly of the livelihood he had lost.

I empathized with Hanh and wanted to tell him so, but I felt a need to separate myself, if such was possible, from the role my country played in the misery of his.

My pacifist conscience took the lead.

"I don't believe war is the best way to solve the world's problems, Hanh."

His eyes darted fire in my direction.

I continued. "We sent soldiers to Vietnam to fight, but many young men in our church refused to fight and told the government so."

Hanh looked toward me. "Why you not fight?"

"Because our God tells us to love our enemies, not hate them."

He looked up, puzzled at my response.

"We believe in compassion, Hanh, love and concern for every human being on Earth. We cannot kill people we love."

Changing the subject, I pointed to the stamps.

"Your stamps say eighty cents. How much is eighty cents in Vietnam?"

"To send letter, if I work Vietnam, I maybe get one dollar ef'ery day. I mus' buy food . . . very expansive to send letter."

Wrinkling his brow, he continued. "Bi' father work veddy hard to send two letter. He can not write every week, he say."

I slipped a sidelong glance at the envelopes, then looking at Bi, confused, I said, "Hanh said your father sent these, but I thought your brother and sister wrote them."

"My Daddy, he try write, Chean, but he can not. When he get my letter, he cry, cry, he so happy! Many people lif' country," she added, swooping a large expanse of neighbors and kinfolk into her arms. "They go my family. They say they happy we in Ame'dica now!"

I could only imagine the joy of finally learning that a long-lost daughter, a child whom you loved so dearly, was alive and well after so much time. The emotions of those moments must have mirrored the sentiments of a certain group of disciples when they learned their Master was not dead, but was, indeed, alive.

"My daddy," Bi continued. I couldn't stop her steam-roller enthusiasm for anything now, nor did I wish to. "My daddy, he try write Hanh 'n' me, but he can not. My brother say he too upset. He tell my brother, my sister they mus' write. Tha's why two letter!"

"My sister say on Tet, what you call, 'Chinese New Year' . . . " Bi paused to make sure we heard her. " . . . Hanh mother, she go twenty-five mile to see her. They bring Ngoc My!"

"Ngoc My?"

I felt my pulse rise.

Bi's musical voice sang the refrain she had repeated before. "My baby, she walk, walk, walk . . . she talk, talk, talk! My sister say she pretty!"

Placing the phone on its receiver; inwardly I swallowed my tears.

Adam looked perceptively at me and saw the wispy moisture in my eyes. "Mom," he asked, "why are you smiling funny?"

I snuggled him in my arms and hugged him close for assurance. *Oh, honey,* my heart cried out, *if I thought you were gone forever and suddenly learned you were alive, I would react exactly as I am right now!*

My eyes squeezed shut as I rocked him in my arms.

―◦―

That fall we enrolled My in Headstart, and her English improved dramatically. Occasionally, as Bi and I sat engulfed in conversation, Bi would stop My in her tracks and ask her daughter to define an enigmatic word.

One day, when the family was visiting, Billie caught the little urchin to give her a bear hug. They had barely entered the living room when Billie noticed something nasty: bruises on My's neckline.

Without thinking, Billie accosted Bi,

"Bi, why does My have marks on her throat?"

The little elfin, sensing she was the object of Grandma's displeasure, scuttled out of her chair, but Billie caught her by the dress tail. When My flitted in the opposite direction to escape Grandma's indignation, Billie crossed her legs and captured her squirmy body between them. Tilting the child's chin upward, she noted a chain of black and blue splotches lining her throat.

My's huge black eyes flitted across the room to her mother, then back again to Gramma. Bi cowered lamely under Billie's displeasure, sulking timidly into the background.

Mommy America was dumbfounded. She couldn't believe what she saw. She thought Bi was beyond inflicting bruises on a four-year-old.

"Bi, why did you do this?"

"Mommy," Bi answered, "My haf' sore t'roat."

Bi rubbed her fingers together in pinching fashion.

"When My don' get well, I do this. Next day if t'roat sore again, I do again. My haf' sore t'roat two week. Medicine don' help. I don' know what do, so I do like Vietnam."

Catching Mommy America off guard, Bi's eyes betrayed her innocence.

Billie shook her head in wide-eyed astonishment.

Maybe the folklore or witchcraft, whatever one wanted to call it, was successful in Vietnam, but logic told Billie that, in a normal week or two, with proper care, a sore throat would have disappeared. Yet this is what the young mother thought, and Billie had to deal with it.

Billie paused, trying to retract her indictment, "Bi, honey," she said, "in America when child is sick, we give medicine. If medicine doesn't help, we go to the doctor. We do not do this."

Billie twisted her fingers to emulate how Bi likely had inflicted the bruises.

"But, Mommy," Bi cried, "I try help My!"

"I know you tried, but this . . . " Billie pointed toward the bruises. "does not help her! If My's teacher sees it, she will say Bi is a bad mother. Same, same, doctor!"

Mommy America sighed, eager to make an end to this embarrassing, but necessary, lesson. "Listen, Bi," she said, "do what I tell you. My must wear shirts with high collars until the marks on her neck go away. Let's go to the bedroom and get one now!"

Bi followed Mommy like a wounded puppy, her feelings deeply assaulted. How was she to know what Americans used for medicine?

Noting her distress, Billie whirled around and hugged her.

"Bi, it's all right. You didn't know better."

But it was too late. Bi was sobbing now. She had betrayed Mommy America, her link between her old life and the new.

"Mommy," she gasped, frightened. "You send me back, Vietnam?"

The question sent a shock wave through Billie.

"Oh, no, Bi! " Billie shouted. "A thousand times over, NO!" Oh, how could she have hurt Bi so? She didn't mean to do that!

The coiffured grandma pulled the young mother to her chest and let her sob. She seemed so small and vulnerable.

"Bi," Billie whispered, exasperated at her inability to communicate with the young mother. "We'll never send you back! You're in America now!"

With that, she leaned over and kissed Bi's tussled hair.

◄o►

A few days later, Clara Etta dropped Bi and the children off at the parsonage. The three of us spent the morning studying English. After an hour or so, we relinquished the chore to tomorrow and relaxed with a glass of sun tea.

The warm day left a dewy freshness in the out-of-doors. As we sank into our easy chairs, sun flooded the living room. I slid open the window, and a rush of fresh air, accompanied by robin song, swept into our chamber.

MiRan and Tuan whooped through the room and into the kitchen, carting tinker toys and Lincoln logs on a plastic wagon. Tumbling over each other, they toppled their cargo upside down on the grass-green carpet.

◄o►

"You know, Bi," I said as we sank into the sofa, "Hanh's birthday is October 1st, right? It's coming soon."

"Why you say 'bir'day?" she asked.

I glanced askance at Clara Etta, who appeared somewhat surprised.

Looking toward Bi again, I said, "In America we give gifts to people on their birthdays. Don't you give gifts in Vietnam?"

"No," she said, tossing the black waves across the nape of her neck.

"Birthday not so important." Her eyes dropped low, as though her culture fell short of something innately special.

Suddenly, I recalled that Bi had no birthday when she came to the states.

I grasped the arm of her chair. "Bi, let's have a birthday party for Hanh!"

"Great idea!" Clara Etta concurred. "What would he like for a gift?"

I squinted my eyes, trying to remember. "Bi, didn't you bring a few pictures from Vietnam?"

Shaping a large square in the air with my hands, I added, "Maybe we could enlarge a special one for his birthday."

Bi disappeared into the hallway, then re-appeared bearing three snapshots, one of them as a couple, another of their wedding day, and the third one of Hanh's family.

"Which one does he like best?" Clara Etta mused.

Bi debated between the wedding picture and his family photo. At first, she handed me one, and then retrieved it. Shuffling through them a second time, her emotions conflicted her. Finally, she gave me the other.

"This one, Chean." She handed me the wedding photo and slid the others in their packet.

Not as confident as she, I asked again, "Are you sure Hanh would like this one best?"

"No," she drawled. "I think he like this one." She handed me the family photo.

I winked at Clara Etta as Bi disappeared into their bedroom with the rejected picture.

"At least, we'll know what to get her for Christmas!"

—◄o►—

We took a break, and Bi joined the children on the floor. They were busy building a tinker-toy tower with windmills and superfluous appendages.

Bi gave one of the windmills a whirl, and Clara Etta burst out laughing. "This brings back memories of my childhood!" she said, the little girl of her youth sparkling in her eyes. "Back then, I played ball in the backyard with my children!"

Her eyes widened as she turned in Bi's direction. "I had five of them, you know!"

Bi imbibed the meaning of her words. "Bi haf' five children, too!" she said.

I glanced at Clara Etta with fire in my eyes. "My goodness!" I retorted. "Do you think she does?"

The experienced grandmother leaned over, placed her hand on Bi's, and calmly said, "Tell me about them, Bi."

The slender lady with the dark wavy hair counted them on her fingers. "My, Tuan, Ngoc My in Vietnam wit' Hanh's parents, 'n'...her eyes looked askance at me..."two babies die, one Vietnam, one Malaysia."

Unpleasant thoughts were more than I needed this day. I didn't want to deal with it so, impolite as it seemed, I redirected the subject. "Tell me, Bi, does Hanh have brothers and sisters?"

"Yes," her huge eyes lifted to mine. "He haf' two sister, Co Op and Co By. They on picture, Chean!" She pointed them out in the snapshot of Hanh's family. Four figures posed in front of a thatched roof structure. His mother sat to the right of center clothed in a long, dark frock. The father stood beside her at the left. Over the mother's right shoulder hovered two lovely young women.

Bi peered at the lady dressed in white. "This Co Op," she said. "She get marry after we leave Vietnam."

Her thin finger swung across the photo to the other sister, a pretty girl of 23 or, maybe a year or so older. The kindness in her countenance beamed a radiant message.

"Co-By," Bi continued. "She will not marry. Two young men, they like her veddy much 'n' want marry her. She say 'No!' She will live wit' Mother an' Father an' take care Ngoc My." Bi huffed her mouth in a mock pout. "Co By veddy luf Hanh 'n' me. She tell Hanh parents she stay wit' Ngoc My."

We chuckled at Bi's acting shenanigans, but were veritably touched by the devotion of Hanh's sister.

Bi turned her head toward Clara Etta. "I haf' question. You say you haf' five children. In America, I see many wit' two, t'ree. Why? Many people Vietnam, same-same Bi.

Clara Etta cast a grin askance at me. "That's a loaded question!" she said.

She shuffled her skirt and pulled her chair sideways to face Bi directly.

"Bi, in your country many babies die. Yes or no?"

"Yes," Bi responded.

Clara Etta continued. "Parents in your country have many babies because some die. They need children to care for them when they get old. In our country, we have Social Security ."

"What you say?" Bi asked, her head turning to catch the words.

Clara Etta grinned, then shuffled, wondering how to explain this. "Everybody works, like Hanh," she said. "We pay Social Security money to the government from our paychecks. The government puts our money into a bank, and it makes interest. When we get old and cannot work, the government gives it back to us. Understand?"

Bi looked perplexed. "Interest?"

Clara Etta went on. "The government bank uses your money to give people loans. When people pay it back, they pay you more because they used your money. We call that 'interest'. Do you understand, Bi?"

Bi nodded.

"Most people save for when they get old. Sometimes their children help, but if the children can't, it's important to save now . . . when you're young. That's Social Security."

I breathed a sigh of relief, glad Clara Etta had this chore instead of me.

I shifted in my chair to bring up another point. "Also, Bi, in America parents do not have so many children. I protruded my hands over my abdomen to indicate a very pregnant woman. We have good doctors when the baby is inside the mother."

"The doctor tells the mother how to take care of herself and her baby. When it is born, it is usually OK. It does not die. Today, if we have two children, then two children will likely live. If three children, then three will live. Sometimes," . . . I raised my hand to point out the exception, "sometimes one dies in America, but not as often as in your country."

Bi turned her head as if to allow the import of our discussion to sink in. It was their decision.

◄○►

The sun shone down on the hot sultry day. It was a lazy afternoon, certainly an inauspicious one. Bi had graciously volunteered to keep MiRan so the children could play.

I flipped the pages of my magazine. Ahhh, the joy of reading without interruption! What more could a busy mother want?

The phone clattered beside me. I lifted the receiver, still engrossed in my article. "Hello, Smiths," I answered halfheartedly.

It was Bi.

"Chean! Come my house . . . now!"

"What's wrong?"

"You come now!" she repeated, emphatically. "Bicycle . . . big man . . . veddy angry . . . come NOW! Please!

Her pointillist rendering between breathless gasps didn't leave me with much to go by, but a fiery alarm sounded in my brain.

MiRan is there! I thought. *Does it have to do with the children?*

"I'll be right over, Bi," I said, my quivering voice struggling to retain composure.

In the car, I sped across town, afraid to face the problem, realizing that promptness was of utmost importance. Jumping out of the car, I ran to their apartment. Not bothering to knock, I pushed through the door. There sat the three little urchins, one to a chair, wide-eyed and frightened.

Bi's customary shyness gave way to the urgency of the moment. Her face was pale and her troubled eyes squinting. Her hands shook with a continuous tremor as she brushed the hair back from her forehead.

"Man, he come here, Chean, big man! He do like this!" Her clenched fists throbbed back and forth toward me, as if to attack. "He angry, veddy angry. I don' know why."

Bi's fright and confusion were obviously apparent.

The children's faces told me they knew more than Bi did. I promptly hunched down on my knees so I could look them squarely in the eyes.

"What happened, MiRan?" She was my best source of information since she could interpret, but she froze like a trapped animal and refused to speak.

My reacted in the extreme the opposite direction. Full of jabbery talk, nothing intimidated her. "Big boy," she chattered excitedly, "We go tricycle! Big boy do this!"

She clenched her fists, just as Bi said the man had done. My rattled on, but in the midst of her excitement, I couldn't make sense of the rest of her story.

There was only one way to learn the truth. We must find this man and talk. I grasped the children's hands and marched with them to a row of apartments in the adjacent building.

"Which one?" I asked.

My's wide eyes betrayed a glassy horror, her little fingers cold and trembling in my hand. Intimidated, she chirped, "Over there."

Not knowing what to expect, we walked over to the apartment and knocked.

My throat tightened when a huge, unshaven man appeared at the door. He whisked a look at the children and emerged through the rusty screen, trailing a sweat-tinged odor. A faded army uniform rumpled on his body as he locked his iron-wrought arms and set his jaw in place, like steel.

Rocking on his heels, his purpling face released a snicker that raised the hair on the nape of my neck. Given his demeanor, I knew I would have to deal with this fellow tactfully, but firmly. There was no room for error.

I braced myself for the worst, but, first, decided to hear him out.

"We have a problem here," I said as calmly as possible. "Can you enlighten me?"

His mouth pulled back in an iron-locked grimace. "Now, look! I wanna tell you something! These three little brats came down here and beat up my boy!"

The cold war had started. I hoped it would stay cold.

"What was your son doing?" I asked. "I can't imagine these three little pre-schoolers beating up on a big kid unless he threatened them," I added.

His brow furrowed in a menacing manner, and abusive language poured from his mouth. He reminded me of a boiler in which the pressure was steadily rising.

"He wasn't doin' nuthin' . . . just sittin' there mindin' his own business, and they attacked him." The hatred reeked from his lips like nourishment for some inner craving.

His demeanor brought out the 'teacher' in me, and I decided to ferret out the truth.

"Now wait a minute," I insisted, "he had to be doing something. We've worked closely with this family for the last six months, and they are not as aggressive as you seem to think."

I peered at him intensely to drive home my point. "If these children did anything wrong, they must have been aggravated."

As I waited for his response, a huge misshapen woman appeared in back of him. She wore a wrinkled shirt and bore several bruises on her face. It suddenly hit me that this guy might be a wife-beater, no one to fool with. As my nerves flexed raw, frailty surfaced inside me, but I squelched my primitive 'flight or fight' demeanor for a phony business-like front.

"Where's your son?" I asked. "May I see him?"

The woman waddled past us outside, over to the edge of the building. Cupping her mouth with her hands, she yelled, "Robby!"

A young fellow, appearing to be eight or nine, flitted around the brick building, hurling verbal abuses to a cohort behind him. When they saw us, the boys stopped short, and then receded.

The big man dropped his hammer-locked arms and pinched up Robby's nose. "Looka this!" he demanded, displaying the evidence of someone's injustice—a scrape on the young man's bridge.

From the looks of the wound, I wasn't sure who was hurt most, Robby or his father. Yet something seemed amiss. The belching anger seemed out of proportion to the wound.

Frightened, MiRan and Tuan clung tightly to my jacket, trembling. I asked My to tell me what happened, but intimidated by her accuser, she retreated.

"When an answer wasn't forthcoming, I said, "I don't understand what happened, but it's clear to me Robby has a scratch."

"A cut!" he injected meanly. "A x#@*&# cut!"

His vulgar language dulled the edge of his nerves, as he spewed his vindication between clenched teeth. "And I'll tell you right now, if anything like this happens again, I'll take things into my own hands!"

His fists clenched again, and something in his voice said the threat was being repeated for a final time.

My maternal instincts hovered over the children behind me.

I set my jaw and spoke. "Just a minute, Mr. ..."

"Rugger!" he fumed.

"Our church brought this family to Bryan, and as far as we're concerned, WE are responsible for their behavior. If anything more happens, and I mean anything," I looked him level in the eyes, "you contact 'us', not 'them'! Do you understand? 'WE' will be responsible. In no way do I want you or anybody else hurling threats at them. You stay away from them, and we'll see that they stay away from you! And that's a promise," I added sternly.

The glint in my eye told him I meant business. And I did.

Then came the unexpected.

The fragile emotions inside the guy began to crumble.

"We've only been here a few weeks," he said. "We don't know what for people lives down here."

His head dropped, and he shifted his massive hulk to the opposite foot. "We had a fire some time back. You probably read about it in the paper."

My mind flew over the last few weeks. I most certainly remembered that fire. As I recalled, it was one in which Bill Hardman helped to retrieve the remains of a tiny, charred body.

"We lost a son in that fire, littler than Robby," he choked.

Mr. Rugger clearly wasn't used to being yelled at, certainly not in recent times. His facial muscles worked back and forth, his eyes so naked with despair that he was embarrassed to return my gaze.

Suddenly the pieces snapped into place. "I gotta watch out for Robby now," his tired voice said. "He's all I got."

I couldn't believe what I was hearing. Mr. Rugger was obviously a desperate man. He needed a vent to lash out his anger—anger at anyone who stepped into his path. The world had swallowed his pride and joy in a blazing, fiery furnace, and he was devastated, emotionally in shambles, in the throes of disorientation.

Mr. Rugger was a man to be pitied, not hated. Yet his irrational frame of mind told me he was, also, a man to be feared, at least until he got his life together.

"I'm sorry," I said and offered him my hand. "I had no idea. But you will call us if you have any further problems with the children?"

"All right," he said, disarmed.

We left, assured of his word.

The children and I returned to the apartment. Hanh arrived home from work, and Billie, who dropped by, pursed her lips when we told them.

"What happened?" she asked, fearing our heyday had come to an end.

"I'll explain it to Hanh and Bi first, Billie. Then you'll understand."

The muted couple looked dwarfed as their frightened eyes followed me around the room. How could I explain a concept as complex as 'psychological transference' so that they could comprehend it?

I opened my mouth and the words fell out at random. "Bi, the man's house burned down three weeks ago. His family had a fire."

"Fire?" she asked.

She intoned a question to My, who translated for her.

Bi stared at me, perplexed. "Fire?"

She had reaped a host of angry words from the ill-tempered tyrant, but what had they to do with 'fire'?

"Bi, the man had a son—little, like Tuan—who died in that fire. He feels badly about it."

Hanh listened in a state of stupor, obviously worried for the safety of his family. Personally, I was, too.

I continued. "The man is angry at everybody, every thing. When the children hurt his son, he became very angry."

The look in her eyes told me that the fellow's emotional upheaval was more complex than they realized. And so it was.

"Bi, I told the man that My and Tuan will not bother him anymore. He lives in the next building." Gesturing toward the south, I added, "You must tell your children, and I will tell MiRan, that they must not go near that building anymore. The next time he might hurt them."

Hanh's eyes met Bi's. I knew the lesson would be taught.

The case cared for, I turned to Billie. "The only thing I don't under-stand is why My and Tuan acted as they did. It was so unlike them."

Billie's mind began to click. "Tell me, Jeanne, did that boy have sandy colored hair?"

"Yes, he did," I answered.

"And was he about this high, maybe nine or ten?"

I gazed at her, astonished.

"Yes. Why?"

"Then he must be the one who's been taunting them these last couple weeks. There's a boy, no more than third or fourth grade, who stands outside their apartment and calls the children "dirty little Japs" and "dirty little niggers.""

"Oh, Billie," I lamented.

"Yes," she shook her head. "I've heard him say it myself. It's true."

◄o►

"You dirty little Japs! You dirty little niggers!" Herb intoned from the pulpit the following Sunday.

The incident so seared the prejudice that adults too often imprint on their children that Herb scrapped his sermon for another that bubbled from the depths of his soul. He, too, pitied the man, as I did, but he found no ex-cuse for the barbaric values he transmitted on innocent people.

What was Herb's contention? That no one, absolutely no one, regard-less of race, creed or color should be sacrificed as a scapegoat on the altar of intolerance. For One had already been sacrificed two thousand years ago, and that was One too many.

Hanh and Bi escaped the holocaust of that sermon. They occupied the pew beside Billie and Earl as they usually did that Sunday, but they fingered meticulously a letter handed to them only minutes before the service. It came from Hanh's cousin in Saigon via the church's mailbox.

I had worried about the tidbits of Herb's sermon that they might catch that morning, for they surely would have recognized the incident. But, feel-ing church too sacred a place to tear open the envelope, they simply stared at it, turning it over and over for hints of the message inside.

A few minutes into the sermon, they could bear it no longer, and Hanh quietly ripped the short edge of the envelope open with a pencil. He gently tilted it to slide out the letter inside, and out dropped a photo of Ngoc My with Co By.

They were spared the heartache of Herb's sermon as their hungry eyes feasted on tangible evidence of their baby daughter, Little Girl Lost.

22
Celebrations

Birthdays, Fourth of July

Hanh banged on the front door of our white frame parsonage. He wore a lightweight jacket in the chilly evening air. We never could understand why he dressed as he did. He wore woolen caps in summer and cardigans in cold weather. It almost seemed he had a psychological need to defy the extremities of our Ohio weather. Billie and I figured he wasn't hurting anybody so we didn't worry about it.

Herb answered the door. "Hello! Come in, Hanh!"

"No," Hanh beamed. "You can let me drive car?" A friend stood beside Hanh, a fellow in his twenties. "This my friend from Lao, Hub." Hanh never could quite pronounce his r's correctly.

Herb offered his hand to the friend. "Glad to meet you," he said.

We knew there was another refugee family from Laos in our small town. Per our request before conference that summer, they were sponsored by the Methodists in Bryan. However, after Hanh and Bi had an initial rendezvous with them which resulted in frustration because they spoke different languages, we didn't create opportunities for them to visit.

'The boy Lao,' as Hanh called him, was fairly adept at English, but now that Hanh's mastery of English improved, the young man frequented their apartment. He even asked Hanh to find him a wife.

Not knowing how to respond, Hanh asked Earl to help him.

Earl shook his head and sighed. "Hanh, I don't know anybody. He will have to find his own wife."

And, then, as an afterthought, Earl rolled his eyes and added, "Tell him he's in America now!"

◄○►

Bi's thriftiness finally reaped results, and Billie helped the family set up a payment plan for a used car with a salesman in our congregation. Pride beamed from Hanh's face when Lee handed him the keys to his newly purchased '73 Buick. The lack of insurance prohibited him from driving the vehicle out of the church parking lot, but he spent a good two hours a week or more driving it back and forth, changing gears, and learning how to maneuver it.

Earl occasionally allowed Hanh to drive the Kornrumpf car on the road since he was very careful. However, the outings were fairly nerve-racking because Earl had an underlying fear that Hanh might misunderstand a quick, but critical command.

In the meantime, Hanh biked to church and practiced driving in our parking lot. The brown Buick became so familiar to parishioners that, when Hanh finally received his license and drove around town, the vehicle stuck out like a lavender Cadillac, resulting in friendly waves and horn blasts.

-◄o►-

One afternoon, I watched Hanh through our parsonage window as he showed his car to the young man from Laos. It occurred to me that a latent teenage frenzy might overcome his better judgment, but I trusted Hanh.

With his friend at his side, he protruded the jangling keys and opened the passenger door with a flourish. Sticking his head inside the car door, the friend leaned one arm on the upholstered seat and fingered the dashboard with the other. Representing a tangible symbol of independence and self esteem, the car appeared a luxury to him, beyond his wildest dreams. Indeed, it was for Hanh since he was now the financial support of his household.

The friend slid into the seat on the passenger side, and Hanh strutted around the vehicle like a proud parent. He deposited himself behind the wheel, flicked on the ignition, and for an hour they drove back and forth, back and forth, in the parking lot.

-◄o►-

"Happy Birthday!" Herb laughed as he seized Hanh's hand, pumping it up and down.

I strutted past the surprised guest of honor with the birthday cake and a sneaky grin. The children clamored at my feet, while Bi exuded pride in her husband.

Bob and Fern followed on my heels with a block of white cheddar cheese, and Florence flaunted the ice cream. Jerry and Sharon tugged a cooler with soda, while others brought the rest of the feast. Eighteen of us streamed into their apartment that Thursday night after work.

Elated at the turn of events, Hanh asked, "You like music, Vietnam?"

Without waiting for an answer, he twisted the volume on his tape recorder. It belted out a loud, pulsating whine. Trying not to notice the rhythmic moan, we strained to hold a conversation over the din. As the minutes metamorphosed into pandemonium, Fern discretely slipped to the back of the group and tactfully laced her fingers over the boom box until she found the controls. Gradually, she inched the sound lower and lower until she found an excuse to flick it off altogether.

Taking advantage of the reprieve, Sharon laughed out loud, "Hey, everybody! Let's sing 'Happy Birthday' to Hanh!"

Shouts and cheers flashed around the room like an electric current. The air charged with delight when Blanche tottered to the middle of the floor with a fully lit birthday cake.

A dozen persons harmonized the birthday song to a half dozen different pitches, but the lively spirit in which it was sung compensated for our lack of talent. Someone grabbed Hanh from the rear of the company and boosted him headlong into the center of attention amidst a generous abundance of laughter.

The music warbled to a high elastic pitch, then modulated down again. We had no more gotten through than Jerry called out, "Another verse!" We continued singing, vying for the world's worst or loudest chorus, I didn't know which. Certainly we could have won the zaniest, for numerous voices screeched above and droned below the scale, all of them on purpose. The last note faded away, and before the tumult began anew, a deep base crooned, "And many moooore!"

Again, we burst into clamor. Herb seized Hanh's hand with both of his and pumped it.

Finally, a host of 'sh-h-hs' silenced the room. Hanh stood staring at the cake, not knowing what came next. An awkward silence filled the room, and I noticed an uneasy question in his expression. Others must have seen it, too, because the prolonged silence became even more pronounced until someone, eager for action, hooted, "Blow out the candles, Hanh!"

The tension released, everyone broke again into raucous laughter while Hanh looked questioning at the candles. The children demonstrated lively puffing to show Hanh what came next.

"Hanh, don't you have birthdays in Vietnam?" Wilma called from the back of the room.

"No!" Hanh shouted over the din.

Tuan demonstrates how to blow out candles on his dad's birthday cake.

Jerry attempted to control the ruckus. "Hey, quiet down, everybody!" Hanh wants to say something!" It worked, partially.

The guest of honor laughed. "Tha's OK! Ef'rybody, talk, talk, talk! You have goot time my house tonight!"

"What do they do for birthdays in Vietnam?" someone quipped.

Doug ignored the interference and spoke directly to the guest of honor. "Hanh, it's your birthday. What do you have to say!"

Hanh surveyed the group and saw a captive audience. Destined to come up with an answer, he responded. "In Vietnam, nobody haf' birthday like this," he gestured with a wave of his hand. "Ef'rybody haf' birthday on Tet. He looked to his wife. What you say, Bi?"

"New Year. Chinese New Year," she explained. "Ef'rybody birthday, same-same."

Adam and MiRan darted their eyes back and forth.

"Do you like birthdays, Hanh?" someone teased.

"Yeah-h-h!" His eyes twinkled, as pandemonium broke loose again.

Somehow we managed slivers of cake and meager dips of ice cream garnished with a notable pot-luck.

Hanh liked the enlarged picture we gave him and gawked at it until his hungry eyes could feast no more.

Moments before we left, teacher Mabel arrived at the door. She stumbled into a room teeming with people on chairs, people on the sofa, people on benches, and others on the floor. Stepping through an entanglement of arms and legs, she chuckled at the unexpected reception, as a plate of cake and ice cream wobbled from one hand to another in her direction.

An hour or so later, by ones and twos and fours, we reluctantly bid the family farewell. As Herb locked our children in their seatbelts, I overheard Hanh asking Earl, "Daddy, why church people so goot to us?"

Closing the car doors behind us, I knew what Earl would say: "Because our God tells us to love you, Hanh. Because our God tells us to love you."

◄O►

Hanh despised his new teeth. The oral surgery went well, but with the exception of chewing meat, he had few complaints. For the first time in months he ceased sniffing eucalyptus to deaden the pain. The dentist had more problems than Hanh did, though, for he lost the mold and had to make a new one. The delay took five more weeks. It might not have been so bad, but all Hanh could eat was soup, soup, and more soup.

Stepping out of the dentist's office that day, Hanh wrenched his new teeth in a lateral direction. When that failed to alleviate the problem, he worked his jawbone to and fro until I feared his dentures would flip out and fall into the gravel. When I left him in front of their apartment, he was grinding, snapping and rolling his jaws in circuitous motion.

On Halloween evening, Herb and I invited Billie and Earl to dinner. Hanh and Bi came, too, complete with a lively My and Tuan. The children soon disappeared into the toy room with Adam and MiRan.

When the little ones finally emerged for dinner, they had mischievous smiles on their faces. The toy room was a disaster. A dozen innocent dolls lay in a row, individually wrapped for bedtime. An assortment of books were scattered helter-skelter, and tinker toys were sprinkled like pick-up sticks across the carpet.

With dinner imminent, all four tumbled, racing to the table. 'Gramma Billie' snatched Tuan to scold him, but his stubby legs continued to jog when suspended in mid-air.

The only silence of the evening was Hanh's. He perched at the table, picking at his food and barely eating. I glanced at Billie and saw she noticed, too. Earl tried to tease him into a better mood, but Hanh refused to respond with anything more than a casual grunt.

"Your teeth hurt, don't they?" Billie asked.

"Yeah," he moaned, rubbing a hand over his swollen jaw.

"Didn't the last visit correct your problem?"

"No. Still hurt," he groaned miserably.

We tried to console him with the notion that he had only to agonize a few more days until the two week adjustment ran its course. We might as well have informed a hungry person that food was only two weeks in coming.

Soon after dinner, the four urchins metamorphosed into Mickey Mouse, a fairy princess, Batman, and Tweety Bird. A little later, I drove the children with Bi and Hanh to a nearby neighborhood where a number of our members lived. We parked the car and started our escapade up and down the sidewalks.

One lawn boasted flashing strobe lights, illuminating a mechanical ghost bobbing up and down. A makeshift graveyard, complete with an animated corpse in its coffin, appeared, then disappeared from sight. A household of teenage boys who outgrew 'Trick or Treat', but who were still intrigued by the holiday, enjoyed creating these bazaar experiences.

The children pulled Bi and me into a phantom playground where we witnessed yet another devil. Sporting the skeletal head of an overstuffed effigy that it had decapitated, eerie hollow music floated over the block, beckoning other miniature monsters to gravitate in their direction.

Hanh sat in the car nursing his dentures while we traipsed with the children from one door to another. Bi and I kept watch from the sidewalk.

"Twick or Tweat!'" the four chirped. Then, one by one they mumbled their gratitude and scurried on to the next house, satisfied with their sweet offerings.

◄o►

That Monday evening, I promised to help Hanh and Bi study their driving manual. After arriving at their apartment, I hesitated to remind Hanh of our commitment since he was preoccupied with a silent flick of 'The Three Stooges'. For fifteen minutes he guffawed, bellowed, and hooted at the ludicrous antics of the clowns. He so enjoyed his time watching them that I thought he'd split, as he held his aching sides trying to control his pleasure.

I looked at Bi. "Why is Hanh so happy? I thought his teeth bothered him?"

She darted a sheepish glance at him and snickered, "Hanh, you tell Chean why you laugh."

Hanh squinted his almond eyes, and then, he frowned. "What you say? I watch TV."

"Tell Chean about teeth!"

His face jerked around, blushing. "Huh?"

It was his turn to be embarrassed. He looked at me as though I knew more than I actually did. Then, he coyly grinned. "I take teeth like this," he said, jerking the imaginary porcelain from his mouth. Settling into his chair, he stated flatly, "I don' like!"

Hanh never did adjust to the confines of those dentures. He concealed them in Bi's sewing basket and brought them out of hiding only for church suppers and special company. The remainder of the time, he ate soft foods— soup, soup, and more soup!

23

Straight! Red light! Stop here!

Learning to Drive

"Snow? What you say, Daddy?" Bi's wrinkled brow searched Earl's expression as she stacked the dishes.

"Hanh! Tell your wife about snow," Earl demanded.

Hanh secretly gloated in Daddy's attention, but had no idea what he was talking about.

"I cannot say about snow," he admitted.

Billie winked at Earl and chuckled benignly. "Snow is very cold. It gets high, high, like this" She measured drifts looming as high as her chest.

Hanh shot a desperate look toward Bi, who caught her breath and doggedly announced, "I will not go ou'side in snow!"

Billie bustled her shoulders. "Yes, you will, little girl! We'll throw you out!" she teased.

"No, you say is cold!" Bi protested, convinced they meant what she heard.

"Yes! It will be very cold!" Earl forced a convulsive shiver as he wrapped his torso with his arms.

Hanh's voice grew serious then. "It get cold, I cannot work," he stated flatly.

Billie realized, with a start, what they had done so she retreated quickly. "Earl, we've got to quit teasing them. We're just asking for trouble."

Earl looked furtively at Billie, then found himself in compliance. "Hanh, you must go to work."

"No . . . I cannot, Daddy!"

"You must or you won't have a job."

High cheekbones underlined Hanh's dark eyes. "Daddy, I worry snow come. You can teach me drive tonight?"

"Ahhhh!" Earl leaned back heavily in his chair. "I wanted to relax after Bi's good meal, but since you asked . . . "

Hanh's eyes widened hopefully.

Earl gazed fondly at his son, quelling the impulse to say 'no', and then, he changed his mind. Digging into his pocket as a penance for his teasing, he threw the car keys to Hanh. "Okay, Hanh. Let's give it a try!"

Hanh's smiling eyes twinkled as he broke into a grin.

"T'ank you, Daddy."

Hanh's ability to handle the car surpassed Bi's. Bi's style was herky-jerky, an impulsive 'fly-through-the-window' type of driving. One or two hair-raising sessions in the church parking lot convinced Earl that he should teach Hanh first. Then Hanh could instruct Bi after he received his license. Bi reluctantly accepted the decision, but her spirits suffered as she watched her husband steer the car out of the driveway leaving her behind.

━◄○►━

A few weeks later, Hanh became the victim of a two-month layoff. Intent upon keeping the family economically self sufficient, Billie helped them jostle their budget to meet their basic needs.

"Insurance, $5. Groceries, $40. Rent, $45. Bi ... what did you do with the rent money?" Billie called out. "You should have $90 saved by now!"

"Hanh do it, Mommy. I tell him 'no', but he do," Bi answered reticently.

"Hanh, come here!" Billie demanded, her desk buried in an array of bills, envelopes and dollars.

Hanh sauntered to her side.

Billie raised her eyes and met his. "What did you do with the money, Hanh?"

"I put here," he conceded defensively, pointing to his pocket.

"Hanh, you cannot do that. You must put $45 into rent every week or you will have no place to live."

Hanh stared at Billie, unable to decipher.

"What you say, Mommy?"

Billie raised her brows. "I'm telling you, Hanh, the man will say you can not live here if you don't put money in the envelope every week. You must have $90 by now."

Hanh waved his hand toward Bi, his feelings slightly bruised.

"I don' know," he grumbled. "Tell my wife. She can do." He turned to leave the scene, not nearly as repentant as Billie felt he should be.

Bi shifted her eyes uneasily.

"Mommy, I can do. I do money, Vietnam. I can do in Ame'dica, too.

But, Hanh, he don' know. When he put money in envelope, he don' listen to me, but I mus' listen to him."

Bi's speech echoed an unquestioning loyalty to her husband even when she knew he was wrong.

"Hanh!" Billie called across the room, ready for a second round.

"Yeah?" he answered over the blare of the TV.

Billie's eyes flickered impatiently. "You let Bi do the money! Bi does it right!"

"OK," Hanh groaned, his disinterested voice curving around the corner. "Bi can do."

—◦—

We veered across double yellow lines, toppled over guard rails, and bashed into the sides of oncoming cars.

In my dreams I heard myself yelling, "Hanh! Brake! Stop!" as he drove headlong into the path of an oncoming vehicle, while quipping absent-mindedly, "What you say?"

I lay awake several nights deciding how best to proceed. It would be best if Hanh could take all of his driving lessons in the same car, either mine or someone else's, so he wouldn't confuse the controls. And he needed consistent times set aside for lessons, just like his English classes.

—◦—

Snow threatened daily now. Frozen layers of frost etched across stubbles of dead grass, melting later each morning. It seemed ridiculous that his car would sit in our parking lot through the winter with nothing better to do than rust. English kept Hanh occupied for an hour or two each day, but he became restless as he sought impatiently for meaningful activities.

Anticipating Hanh's reaction to the extended layoff at the factory, Bi's eyes grew wide. "You mean Hanh home ef'ry day now, Chean?" She didn't know if she looked forward to it or not.

I was baffled, too, not about his layoff, but about teaching Hanh to drive. What did I know about teaching him driver's ed?

That night I lay awake listening to the clock tick away the hours and decided that Billie's advice given months ago was best: "Choose your words carefully. Simplify, simplify, simplify! Omit the excess clutter. Review maneuvers before hitting the road. Use consistent gestures and make sure he understands them. Encourage him when he does well. But most of all, impress on him the fact that driving, as the most dangerous activity Americans do, should not be taken lightly."

—◄o►—

To my great relief, Hanh's real-life behaviors were antithetical to my harrowing dreams. He was slow and deliberate as a driver, so slow at times that I wanted to jump out and push the car to give it a little shove.

The first day I planned to practice with him for a two-hour block of time but found myself frazzled after one. To be honest, though, all we did was curve back and forth over the half mile stretch of road in our city park.

On the second day, I instructed Hanh to pull into a side driveway to locate the training area for the maneuverability test. I explained how we would practice parallel parking there when his skills improved.

Hanh perked up, peered over his shoulder, and began to back between the four steel stakes. "This easy for me! This easy!" he exclaimed.

I urgently tried to maintain my calm. "No, Hanh! This is difficult, even for people who drive a long time!"

"I can do! Easy! Easy!" He inched my car back further into the slot.

"Hanh!" I continued, "I've driven a car for seventeen years, and sometimes I still can't do it!"

Ignoring me, he continued to back.

I gritted my teeth to keep them from chattering and mashed my eyes shut, waiting for 'the scrunch'.

First, he worked the wheel one direction, and then, the other.

Heaven forbid! I thought to myself. *If he scratches the Dodge, that'll be the end of his driving lessons! Herb would see to that!*

How Hanh did it, I'll never know, but he manipulated into that tight space through a series of tactical maneuverings that I wouldn't care to repeat tomorrow—and without mishap, too. The rods lined up nicely at all four corners of the car.

I gawked in amazement and breathed a measured sigh of relief. Pointing to the single opening that would fray my nerves the least, I said, "Now, Hanh, go straight through the front two rods. Then we can drive in the park."

"No, I do this again!" he said, determined to back up and wiggle his way through the maneuver again.

My knees knocked convulsively, one against the other. When we finally slithered from the spot, I was a mass of tangled nerves.

Sighing deeply and thankful it was over, I said, "OK, Hanh, we can drive to town to practice now."

"No, we do this again," he crowed, proud of his first endeavor. "I drive backward again!"

My hair stood straight on end as he threw the gears into reverse and pumped the brake. The posterior end of the car crept rearward and switched adroitly into the narrow slot. I don't know how he did it, but he did.

The car puttered contentedly as Hanh beamed, but I felt like a frightened rabbit frozen in my shoes. Yet the evidence of his success was real. There was no doubt about it. Hanh knew what he was doing.

"Hanh, many people have trouble when they 'go back', but you backed twice!"

As my reward he pulled out straight and spared me the anguish of another maneuver. After circling the park, he drove me home. That was one of the longest hours of my life. God bless driver's ed teachers!

—◄o►—

In spite of my neurotic sensations thirty minutes before each driving session, I managed to suppress my urgent desire to flee anywhere except 936 East Wilson Street. Once convinced that Hanh could, indeed, parallel park better than I, we spent more time behind the wheel. Our daily lessons consisted of "Signal left! . . . Signal right! . . . Straight! . . . Red light! . . . Stop here!"

The commands seemed endless. Consistent practice and repetition of the same maneuvers were the goal of every lesson. Finally, we graduated to the four-lane street downtown.

"Hanh, we're driving in town today. Are you ready?"

"Yeah," he proffered, eagerly.

I slid a chair from under the table and began to sketch a map.

"What you do, Chean? Don' we drive today?"

I didn't look up, but said, instead, "Come here, Hanh."

He pulled out a chair beside me.

"Now this is the left turn lane." I traced the arrow in the appropriate direction. "When you turn, check your mirror, signal left, and then move into this lane. Then, wait for traffic and . . . make your turn!"

I swung my pencil across the paper completing the perfect maneuver.

—◄o►—

Hanh learned his lesson well that day. In fact, during our session it was apparent that he over-learned it. Swerving the car from the extreme right side, he cut left across two lanes and whooshed into the turning lane all in one swipe.

"Hanh, what are you doing!?!" I barked.

"I do what you say, Chean," he piped, inching around the corner gingerly.

"Signal right!" My arm flew up methodically "Pull over here!"

He obeyed.

"I do some'ting wrong, Chean?"

"Well," I laughed nervously, "Yes and no. Your turn was good, but the lanes, whew!

I pulled out a tablet and scribbled a birds' eye view of the road, then proceeded to enlighten him.

◄○►

Gray clouds darkened the November sky. After Bi's English lesson in the kitchen one day, we waited patiently for Hanh who was helping Bill cut wood.

Bi examined my swollen eyes.

She could see I had been crying. When I told her why, the words tumbled from my lips. "A little boy in Adam's class at school, his father died last night. We went to the funeral parlor to see him. Do you understand me, Bi?"

Bi nodded. She understood. She didn't speak, but listened, listened to the remorse I felt for my friend's husband.

This was not my parents' generation. It was the demise of mine. Our time had come, and I wept for all of us. I sorrowed for the vacuum of years they could not spend together and for the vague empty space yawning in the hearts of his wife and children.

Bi heard my grief, and I was grateful.

◄○►

Soon, the twittering of rain stepped aside, making way for a shower of flurries. Though fresh falling snow mirrored my numb emotions, the tears of my loss felt as hot as the summer sun.

Fluffing my disheveled hair, I streaked the pain across my cheeks and decided to leave.

"Bi, I must go now. The roads are getting slippery."

She sailed to the window and drew back the drapes. Her countenance brightened at the sight of snow.

Her reaction was not what I expected. We had, after all, implanted visions of five-foot drifts in her mind. Still, the scanty flurries did not disappoint her.

The late afternoon light glowed on her almond cheeks as a smile crept across her face. She turned to me.

"Chean, I don't see before! This I don' see!"

I gazed at the piddly offerings of the overcast sky and yearned desperately for it to snow to the rooftops. I wanted for Bi the rare and crazy experience of shoveling a tall, narrow tunnel through the snow to her front door. I wanted to be on the other side of that window smashing slippery snowballs down the glass with her and the family laughing lustily inside. The 'child' in me yearned to play that day. There was too much 'adult' that afternoon.

But reality does not quit easily. Instead, I said, "It's getting slippery, Bi, so I must go."

For the moment, Bi didn't care. The radiance in her eyes fluttered softly to the ground with the quiet snowflakes.

—◁o▷—

"Jeanne, I don't think we should wait any longer. I'm worried about Bi's health." Billie's words came out more like a question than a statement.

I, too, had noticed Bi's melancholy and weigh loss. She was down to ninety pounds. She complained of headaches nearly every day and, more recently, had vomited blood.

"We had better take her to Dr. Moats," I concurred.

—◁o▷—

Dr. Moats peered over Bi's records and scratched his head. "I honestly don't know what to make of this," he confessed. "Her symptoms baffle me."

Relaxing his elbows on the desk, he studied Bi's X-ray in the window light.

He waved us over to examine it with him.

"The TB check is clear. Can you see?" he asked. ". . . but her symptoms aren't severe enough to require hospitalization. I'm going to take a stool sample to check for parasites," he added, more to himself than to us.

We followed the doctor down the corridor to the lab. He emerged moments later with a little brown bag and a few words of instruction.

—◁o▷—

In the car at last, Bi looked to me for an explanation.

"I'll explain when we get to your house, Bi." I said. Procrastination gave me time to think.

At their apartment I pointed toward the restroom. "You go to bathroom, Bi."

"Yeah?" she replied, a look of surprise crossing her brow, as if to say, ' well, isn't that part of the human condition?'

"Every day you go, 'uh-uh'?" I grunted.

"Yeah." She said, confused.

"Dr. Moats says he wants some, three days."

A silly grin crossed her face. "He want?" she twittered.

"Yeah," I nodded my head. "He says he must have for three days."

I withdrew three plastic vials from the paper sack and continued with directions. I couldn't look her in the eye for fear my thin veneer would surface and she'd think that I was joking.

"The doctor says he wants only a little bit, not so much," I explained. But Bi was laughing anyway. If this was what 'American medicine' was all about, this was news to her!

◄o►

A few hours later, Hanh arrived home from work. My scurried to the door to let him in. After shaking the snow from his coat, Bi explained her procedure to Hanh in Vietnamese. I didn't understand what she said, but the expression on Hanh's face ran the gamut from serious to a silly smirk.

Two days later, Dr. Moats issued the diagnosis: An unidentifiable intestinal parasite common in the tropics. A small worm had burrowed into her foot and was carried through the bloodstream to her intestines, due to unsanitary conditions. Bi likely caught it when going barefoot in Malaysia.

The doctor prescribed a potent medication to be taken for three consecutive days by the entire family. I studied the orange box of pills as Bi looked on. At first, I thought we might have to launder linens every day, but the instructions assured us she was not contagious.

Three days passed and Bi passed a parasite. So did little My. But according to My, it was not a mere two inches in length, but all of three feet long. Her eyes bugged out as she described 'the snake' and spread her arms wide to parade its size.

Fortunately, Tuan and Hanh were spared the agony.

24
Freedom to Drive

Hanh's Reward, a "Yellow Paper"

"Hanh, tomorrow let's go for your driving test."

"Goot," the tiny voice percolated on the other end of the line. "What time?"

"Is nine o'clock okay?" I asked.

"Yes."

"Don't forget your permit and the car's registration—everything you need to drive."

He understood the request, mainly because, as the licensed driver during his many lessons, I had made the same request of him numerous times before.

Although Bi's cabin fever sometimes generated headaches, this morning was different. As the easterly sun danced across the glistening clouds outside, her spirits seemed to dance with it. I was delighted with her sudden enthusiasm.

"Mommy want you call her before you go with Hanh, Chean,"

"May I use your phone?"

"Yeah," she answered.

While the Kornrumpf's number was ringing, I said, "Bi, can you come with us? That way, you'll see how it is when Hanh takes the test. Then, if you want a license some day, you'll know what to expect."

"Yeah!" her eyes sparkled. "We come home twelve thirty for My's school bus?"

"Sure. No problem."

I glanced at my watch as she scampered to the coat closet. Then, the anticipated phone call came.

"Billie?" I cradled the phone on my shoulder. "What do you want?"

"How's Bi this morning?" she asked.

"All right, I guess. She seems OK. Why do you ask?"

"I'd better explain something in case she mentions it to you,"
Billie continued. "She called every morning this week with a headache like the ones she had before.

"You mean the headaches she had when they discovered the parasites?"

"Yes. Last night she called me again, but I believe it's tension, thinking about the baby, especially when she can't sleep at night.

"Ahhh, so you think when she settles in for the night, all she can think about is Ngoc My?"

"Right," Billie said. "The doctor thinks so, too. It's taking a toll on her."

Billie began to chuckle, "I told Bi outright, "Now, listen here, young lady!"

I checked the time. We still had a few more minutes. "Billie, is there something I can get you at the drug store while I'm out?"

"No, that's not why I'm calling. Last evening when Bi complained about having a headache again, I told her I was sick, and I was, too. I had a slight fever and was resting. To make a long story short, she thought I got sick because I was worrying about her!"

Billie hesitated. "Don't tell her we talked about this. I'm not sick because of her, but let her think so for a while. If she focuses on me instead of the baby, her doldrums might go into spontaneous remission."

I glanced at the phone, not believing what I heard. Billie was noted for her candid honesty, but never for conniving.

I cradled the phone to my ear. "Whatever you say, Billie. If it's psychosomatic, hopefully, she'll get over it. It would be nice if they could put the doctor's money into the gas tank, instead."

―◁○▷―

A few minutes later, Hanh emerged from the apartment with the fragrance of a heavy application of eucalyptus trailing behind him. He slipped on his coat, and I dangled the keys for him to drive. When he grasped them at one end, I tightened my clutch on the keychain. Our eyes locked, and I injected his psyche with a last bit of advice.

"Hanh, you will do well in the driver's test today. You drove in Archbold and Bryan this week. We spent many hours in the country. You can 'go back' very well. Today the police will look for small details. They are important, so pay attention!"

He stared at me intently, absorbing each word carefully.

I continued. "You must signal right and signal left. Signal every time you turn. When the sign says '25,' then go 25! You cannot go 30. The police will look for mistakes."

"Yesterday, Hanh, you drove in Defiance. Defiance is big compared to Bryan—many cars, narrow streets, red lights, four lanes. If you can drive in Defiance, you can drive anywhere. You'll do well today."

With that, I handed the keys over to Hanh. We had invested a great deal of time and energy in our lessons, and he took my advice very seriously.

Bi and the children perched excitedly in the back seat while I slid in on the passenger side. Hanh positioned himself at the steering wheel and thrust the key into the ignition. He pondered for a moment, sorting the correct moves in his mind. Then, he backed around and coasted out of the driveway towards the police station.

I buttoned my lips, carefully watching his maneuvers. Hanh was on his own now.

◄○►

Thirty minutes later, we entered a cinder block office. The officer sported a stiff demeanor. I didn't know what Hanh was thinking, but outwardly, he displayed a calm exterior.

We followed the officer down a stainless steel staircase, our boots reverberating the tinny sounds of a dungeon. Finally, we emerged outside.

Bi and I stopped short, leaving Hanh to trail the officer. Together, we watched as he revved up the ignition.

The officer sat on the passenger side as Hanh steered to the end of the driveway. The test began.

"Bi," I whispered, "when other people's cars go there, they turn on their signal! Hanh doesn't have his signal on!"

My eyes shot nervously toward hers.

She gasped. "Oh, Hanh, turn signal! Please, Hanh, turn signal!"

She ranted the mantra over and over, as though his mind could assimilate hers through mental telepathy.

"I don't know why he doesn't do it, Bi," I said. I couldn't imagine anything I had taught him more adamantly than that.

Seconds morphed into minutes.

"Why don' he go some place?" she asked.

Finally, to our surprise, he belched across the highway and disappeared down the street.

Squinting my eyes to follow the car, I heaved a sigh of relief. "Look at that, Bi! He didn't need his signal, after all!"

"Goot, goot!" she cheered.

Bi's eyes squinted to catch glimpses of our Dodge passing through tangles of branches. I shrugged my shoulders and shivered in the cool weather. Everything depended on Hanh now.

Soon, he came coasting up the road from the opposite direction. Signaling left, he swerved cautiously into the police station's parking lot and stopped. Inside the car, the officer was explaining something, likely the maneuverability test, to him.

I caught my breath and muttered, "Bi, Hanh can do this, too. He did it for me many times in the park."

Crossing my fingers, I added, "This is for good luck."

Three sets of fingers followed suit.

Watching the car from a distance, Bi strained her neck to watch, smiling through clenched teeth.

"You can do, Hanh!" She shuddered. "Hanh, you can do!"

"Bi's right, Hanh!" I stammered. "Come on, come on! Turn left . . . OK! Now, turn right!"

We sounded like a silent cheering section with our feet nailed to the floor. Though we wanted to cheer him on, common courtesy dictated that we act dignified.

Moments later, Hanh angled his way through the labyrinth, then backed up the car and turned it around.

I heaved a measured sigh of relief.

A few minutes later, the tall officer emerged from the passenger side and proudly announced, "He did very nicely."

I nodded a telltale grin to Hanh while the officer buried himself in routine paperwork.

My stomach fluttered with pride. I fully expected a flare of trumpets to blare, capturing the cop's attention.

The officer glanced up at me. "You're pretty proud of him, aren't you?"

"I sure am."

"You teach him?"

"Oh, he had a couple of teachers, but I helped him the last few weeks."

"Well, he did fine. He seems very responsible," the officer said as he scribbled his signature on the dotted line. Ripping the perforated page from his tablet, he handed the license to me. I stepped aside and nodded for Hanh to take it.

"It's yours, Hanh! You did it!"

Hanh grinned, pleased with his accomplishment, and accepted the yellow paper.

—◀○▶—

Cold weather set in and the lack of snow cooperated beautifully. Hanh proudly drove the family to church on Sundays and even brought them Christmas caroling.

Almost instantaneously, Bi's mental attitude improved. Cold weather no longer sequestered her inside, and Hanh began teaching her to drive.

'Turn right, turn left', the maneuverability test, everything. With prospects of receiving her license, Bi had a new goal, and the housewife doldrums flitted out the window.

Several weeks later, I received a notice in our mailbox.

To: Jeanne L. Smith
"The Bureau of Motor Vehicles of the State of Ohio wishes to inform you that your driver's license expired November 30, 1979. If you wish to renew it, . . . "

I collapsed onto the sofa, aghast. My license had expired the week after Hanh's lessons began! For all my fanaticism as his teacher, I was the offender and never knew it!

25
We Must Give Them "Christ-mass"

Christmas—A Sense of Wonder

Their innocent voices created the chatter of a dozen.

"Mom, can we decorate the tree . . . please?"

When I put off the long-anticipated event, Adam quipped, "Well, then, when can we do it?"

MiRan chimed in with her opinion. "Saturday's too late, Mom! Please?"

I muffled a smile and looked up from the sudsy dishwater into two small pleading faces. The children's innocent yearnings had a way of pricking my conscience.

Had I simply glanced, I might have missed it, but two miniature urchins, their eyes sparkling, were unable to get enough of Christmas.

I knew what I was going to say, but decided, instead, to tease them. "Let's wait 'til Sunday after church. Then we'll have more time."

"Awww, please, Mom? Their sprightly legs danced exuberantly around the kitchen.

I really wasn't ready for it—the lights, the tinsel, the mess, but Adam's countenance mirrored excitement for the task at hand and MiRan's eyes fairly glistened, enrapt with the festive season.

"Well," I drawled, "If you pick up your toys in the living room, maybe!"

I gave them a sidelong glance to accentuate the 'maybe.'

There was an explosion of laughter as the two frolicked around the room. Their pleasure gave way to a sudden course of action as they scrambled into formation. Adam, in the lead, barked orders, while MiRan scooped the incriminating toys up from the carpet. One by one, they hauled them into the playroom and deposited them in the toy chest.

In their zeal to decorate the tree, the exuberance of my children had unloaded an over-abundance of ornaments on the tree's lower extremities. A rope sporting peppermint twirls circumambulated its midriff, while larger ornaments weighed the bottom branches that sagged a little low. Miniature lights sparkling from secret recesses in the foliage framed a homemade crèche as lacy snowflakes dangled from the boughs below.

That week we invited Billie and Earl over for dinner. Bi and Hanh came with them.

Hanh gawked at the tree scintillating in the light. Then, clearing his throat, in a barely audible whisper, he rasped "bou'tiful!"

"Don't you have Christmas in Vietnam?" Billie asked.

"Cwis-mas?" he asked, looking somewhat confused.

"Hanh, do you celebrate Christmas in Vietnam?" she repeated.

"No," he said. "In my house we no have . . . what you say?"

"Christmas," she reiterated.

"Cwis-mas," Hanh repeated. His eyes squinted as he made a sweeping gesture. "In big city, many lights, many people. Children see . . . "

Hanh hesitated, then turned to Bi. "What I say?" Then, as if answering his own question, he added, "*Ong Noi Noem*. He haf' long hair." Hanh gestured downward from his chin, " . . . old man."

I recalled Earl brushing the human fly from his nose at four o'clock one morning.

"*Hanh, Ong Noi*' is 'grandfather', isn't it?"

"Yeah," he answered, surprised that I remembered. "'*Noem*' mean Cwis'mas."

"Grandfather Christmas?" Billie asked.

I slipped back to our storage closet, quickly exhumed a dusty box, and reappeared with a red fur hat and whiskers.

"Is this what you mean, Hanh?"

"Yeah," he beamed. "*Ong Noi Noem*."

"We say 'Santa Claus.'"

'Ong Noi Noem,' he repeated.

Again he emitted 'boutiful,' almost oblivious to our presence.

I glanced at Billie.

Sure, they're Buddhists, I thought, *but why deny them Christmas? Surely, they'll find the Spirit of the Christ in some of our many customs.*

—◦—

MiRan and I scuffled heavily under the weight of winter boots plodding through the snowdrifts. Puffs of warm air from our lungs met the cold and froze before they evaporated. Our muscles tensed against the bitter north wind that seemed to slice through our bodies.

Lowering my head, I cuddled MiRan's tiny face in my scarf. She picked up her gait as we rushed through the drifts into a blast of warmth in the storefront.

The Young Marrieds' class had taken an offering the week before for a tree for Bi and Hanh, and we were on a mission.

Inside the store, we dropped our scarves and shook the cold from our bones. In her eagerness, MiRan grabbed my arm and almost tugged me off balance.

"Mom," she shouted, "they have Christmas trees here! Let's get one for My and Tuan!"

Trailing rivulets of snow behind us, we gazed at two trees perched on a shelf above us. I only had enough money for the four-foot tree, but I could have declared by the miserly size of it that one foot included the lower trunk, and another, the lonely spindle protruding at the top.

"Looks kind of scrawny, doesn't it?" I uttered to myself.

"I like it 'cause it's little!" she whooped, as if assuming the role of counsel for the children in the world.

I glanced down at my self-appointed envoy and tried to swallow my chuckle.

"Get the little one, Mom!" she harped.

MiRan herself was small, her crown of silky black hair scarcely reaching my waist. I glanced at her, then looked at the tree and decided the only difference between the two was that the tree lacked her sparkle.

I vividly recalled her first Christmas with us several years before when she was still a baby. My mother's gift for MiRan that year was a scrawny brown teddy with a little pink nose. Mom's words still echoed in my head: "I couldn't resist buying it because it looked like an orphan."

◄○►

"Excuse me, ma'am," a voice said, as a gurney with long boxes swiveled past us.

"What's in your cart?" I asked.

"Christmas trees."

"What size?"

"Six feet."

"How much?"

"Le' me check."

The worker's eyes darted around, looking for the manager. "Be back in a minute, ma'am," he said.

MiRan looked inquisitively at me. "We gettin' the big one, Mom?"

"Let's wait and see," I answered. She seemed content with that.

◄o►

The manager came, a tall friendly fellow in a blue shirt. "They're $25.00, but if you wait until Friday, they'll be on sale."

"Oh, goodness," I whimpered. "We need it for this evening. We're buying a tree for our Vietnamese family and decorating it tonight."

"Well," he paused. "I'll put a label on it for you so you can get the discount now. How's that sound?"

I nodded in the affirmative and MiRan let out a whoop, while he busied himself clicking his tagger.

We thanked him profusely and left the store with the tree, feeling strangely warmed inside. MiRan and I lilted out the door, our version of a dance under its awkward size and weight. The wind didn't cut as deeply now for the spark of the Christmas season was burning brightly.

◄o►

Bi at Christmas—She is queen of her home.

At precisely 6:00 p.m., like frozen angels out for an evening stroll, a host of church people fluttered into the Nguyens' apartment. Coats skidded from shivering shoulders and huddled in a pile back in Adam's bedroom. A few minutes later, Herb and Verle dragged the tree in and sat on the floor to assemble it.

As the tree built its way toward the ceiling, it showcased garlands of tinsel and a string of colored bulbs. For what is Christmas to a child without the light to reflect the wonder in his eyes?

Clara Etta's colorful packages mimicked the spirit of the season—acrylic icicles, lacquered ornaments, and sequined rosettes. My and Tuan scrambled near her, at a slightly comfortable distance. Though they hesitated to ask what was in the packages, their saucer brown eyes implored her to open them. If the top of the heap glimmered so, what wonderful secrets lay buried beneath it?

Our rowdy bunch quieted momentarily as the tree's lights flickered on. Then everyone broke again into a noisy rabble. Together, we matched hooks and ornaments and dangled them from the splintery greens.

"Yeow!" Tuan squealed, as he bit into a salt cookie meant for decoration.

"Tuan, come out n the kitchen!" Adam chortled. "The real ones are out here!"

Another two made four, and the children heartily downed an unrestrained number of delicacies before Sharon discovered their antics. She steeped a line of cups with a splash of cocoa and marshmallow, and soon the rest of the group intuitively discovered the kitchen.

Finally, all was finished, and we loitered back to the living room, discovering stillness there. The room exuded a mellow glow. We dimmed the lights except for the tree, allowing its warmth to entrance us. Contented, Hanh perched on the arm of the sofa, his large brown hands on little My's shoulders.

Soon, music quelled the atmosphere . . . "Silent night, holy night . . . round yon virgin, mother and child," only to be filled with another carol as the previous one faded.

Across the room, separated by a dozen shadows, Tuan's wondering eyes waved around their circle of friends, then up to his mother who cozied him in her lap.

Looking back in Time, I saw another mother cradling a refugee child of long ago, and I remembered the angels singing just for them.

26
Christmas—A Sense of Wonder

Buddhists Celebrate New Life

The shivery Saturday dawned cold and clear. Adam and MiRan, clad in winter snowsuits, took joy in crashing splintery icicles from the enclosed porch roof with a broom. Starry crystals slid down the glass, streaking the windows outside.

"Hey, Mom!" they bellowed, slamming snowballs against the storm door to capture my attention. Leaving the children to gloat in their fun, I returned to the kitchen, chuckling. It was nice to see them playing together instead of arguing for a change.

On my return trip, Herb was leaning against the bathroom sink, half bearded with shaving cream. He ricocheted a stare at me from the mirror.

"What's so funny?" he asked.

"You," I sputtered. "You look like Santa Claus!"

Herb chased me through the kitchen and into the living room. Grabbing me by both shoulders, he plastered my face with a soggy kiss.

"Serves you right!" he muttered as he returned to the sink.

Moving with new determination, I inched my way closer. I propped my shoulder against the door frame, leaving some leverage between us.

He took a clean, sleek stroke with the razor against his taut neckline. "Insult me again and you're gonna get it!" he fussed.

Retreating a step backwards, I said, "May I ask an innocent question?"

He rolled his eyes at me.

"Don't try any funny stuff now!"

"But this is serious, Herb. We're leaving for Pennsylvania next week to be with our families for Christmas. When can we give Bi and Hanh their gifts?"

He stopped shaving. "What do you mean?" he asked. "Just give them. What else?"

Ahhhh, Vintage Herb! I thought, *systematically boiling everything down to its lowest common denominator!*

Crossing my arms, I came in for a landing. "Do you think they'll be embarrassed if they can't reciprocate?"

He looked up, mustached with a white goatee. Taking a swipe with his shaver-plow, he created a highway across his cheek.

"I don' know.," he said. "Hanh was laid off for a while and they don't have a lot of money."

"Hmmm," he moaned, as he took another swipe. His foam goatee bobbed up and down as he talked.

Stepping backwards into the hallway, I said, "Maybe Howard could help us."

Herb rinsed the stubble from his razor and inspected his chin again. "Howard?"

"Sure, Howard! Blanche could help him get dressed."

Herb acknowledged me with a series of grunts, more interested in his facial bristles than in my conundrum.

"Well, all right . . . go ahead and ask him."

◄o►

"Can you help us, Howard?"

He exuded a throaty chuckle on the other end of the line. "Just a minute," he said, "let me ask Blanche."

Seconds later, he returned. "Sure. What do you have in mind?"

Later that day, we dropped a tattered box at Howard's house on our way to Bi and Hanh's.

When we gusted through the door at the Nguyen household, Hanh was busy whirling a new blender given at his company party the night before.

Bi gave me a quick hug, then, exclaimed, "Chean, look at tree!"

A pile of gifts was nestled beneath it.

Surprised, I asked, "Did you get these for the children, Bi?"

Hanh sauntered in from the kitchen and answered, "One for My, and one for Tuan."

"Only one for each?" I asked.

He explained, "My and Tuan not goot all the time!"

Herb gestured toward the other packages. "But what about these? Who gave these to you?"

Hanh's eyes glinted. "Church people," he said. "Church people veddy luf' us."

Bi flipped the tags, exposing the donors: Betty and Paul, Sharon and Jerry, Blanche and Howard. And how could we forget our Wilma?

And there were others . . . Mary and Blaine, Lois and Paul, and the pile went on . . . Florence and Kedric, Hazel and Harold, and more.

The doorbell rattled, diverting our attention.

My charged headlong toward the entrance. Opening the door, her smile faded to a look of dismay, as she tripped a few steps backwards.

The intruder did not wait for an invitation but barged in uninvited.

"*Ong Gia No En!*"[19] Tuan squealed, as My regained her composure.

The furry Saint Nicholas toted a pillowcase behind him filled with gifts. His large black gloves sported a snow shovel cleverly wrapped with a velvet bow.

Santa emptied the contents of his pouch: a chalkboard for My, Lincoln logs for Tuan, yarn for Bi, jumper cables for Hanh, and their wedding picture, enlarged and framed.

As Santa rose to leave, Hanh jumped to his feet.

"Don' go, Santuh!"

He scrambled to the kitchen and whirled the blender noisily. Moments later, he stalked into the living room with tumblers on a tray. Offering a glass to the guest in red, Hanh suddenly realized the slender Santa might have difficulty imbibing it through his beard.

Santa politely declined the elixir when he observed his plight.

Hanh turned to Herb, and then, to me, offering two more glasses.

I tasted the concoction, then sputtered and nearly choked.

Hanh retreated to the kitchen and returned with smaller offerings for the children. MiRan tasted hers daintily, as though she were at a tea party, then spewed it back in the glass and blurted an embarrassing, "Yuk!"

Shooting Adam a warning with my eyes, he contorted his face to swallow the mysterious concoction, then, he placed his glass on the end table where it remained until we left. Thrusting a glance toward MiRan, I surmised that her mouth was full of something she was wishing wasn't in it.

Herb's eyes darted toward me and read my mind.

Cautiously, I tried to swallow a sip. The liquid seemed palatable enough, but what was the stringy stuff? "Tell me, Bi, what's in this?" I asked.

Before she responded, Hanh emerged from the kitchen with the recipe. There it was, bean sprouts blended with sugar and milk.

The frothy substance was not particularly delectable. In fact, we

---

19 *Ong Gia No En* – Translation: "Old Man Noel" in Vietnamese.

politely asked for forks to fish out the beans between the saccharine swallows. As hard as I tried over the next hour, I could only manage a half glass, one mini-sip at a time.

Santa finally squeezed out the door, somewhat thinner for the lack of "la bean", but his guise did not fool My and Tuan.

No more was the front door closed behind him than the children tackled their presents.

Though Santa stole the show for the kids, judging by the pucker in our mouths, "la bean" stole the show for the rest of us.

◄○►

On Christmas day, we stopped by the family's apartment to wish them a happy holiday. They were anticipating our visit.

Inside, Hanh withdrew a flashy parcel for Adam and brandished another toward MiRan. They ripped the paper to shreds, unveiling toys Hanh purchased at Ohio Art.

"An ironing board!" Ronnie shouted. She flipped the miniature stand on its rack, pretending to press her mittens and scarf.

Adam whirled a colorful tin top on the dining room floor while Tuan's eyes followed its circuitous trajectory.

Hanh pointed to it, proudly. "Workers at Ohio Art, make six t'ousand toy ef'ry day," he said.

Herb squinted, surprised at the volume. Hanh's job on the heavy machine press involved stamping wooden handles around a screw inside of a casing. His foreman told Paul that Hanh was so conscientious he seldom took time for breaks.

Hanh was not one to boast, but he was justifiably proud of his labor. Now that the opportunity presented itself, he felt comfortable sharing his accomplishments.

Bi had two more gifts. "Here, Chean," she grinned.

She must have noticed the tattered condition of my kitchen linens because she blessed me with several new ones, plus a candy thermometer.

Hanh reached for the other parcel and handed it to Herb. Inside was a floodlight "so Hub not fall down when he go church at night."

Perched against the Christmas scene, the family looked complete. Bi was queen in her house now, and she enjoyed it. Hanh stood proud and tall as caretaker of his family.

Bi startled, a thought catching her in transition. Leaning across the sofa, she delved into a box to uncover a tapestry of garden colors woven with tiny stitches.

"I weave, by han'," she said, "for Mommy and Daddy."

"Bi, it's beautiful!" I mused, noting her touch for color.

"But, look, no more t'read. Can Chean find t'read for me?"

She pointed toward the bottom of the tapestry. With only an inch or two to go, she had run out of green.

My mind recalled the hectic hours dashing from one store to another searching for a swarthy hue like the sample she gave me one day.

I looked at her, surprised. "So that's why you asked me to find you some yarn?"

Digging through the clutter in my purse, I extracted three swatches, none of them the right shade.

"Bi" I quipped, "I didn't know you needed these so soon!"

"Tha's all right," she said, "I can do."

Settling into the sofa with the tapestry on her lap, Bi deftly unraveled a few patches of green and replaced them with my off shades. Rich and lush against the threads, her nimble fingers wove the mottled threads into an artistic spectrum.

◄o►

The doorbell rang. Billie's sister, Doris, was there.

The coiffured lady invited herself inside.

Stepping over the Christmas wrappings, she pulled the crinkly foil from her package, revealing a poinsettia intertwined with baby's breath. "These should bloom any time now," she said. "The greenhouse flew them in from Florida."

Billie sat the plant gingerly on an end table while Doris collapsed in an easy chair.

Amidst the din of chit-chat, I vacated my seat and slipped over by the poinsettia.

"Beautiful," I muttered. Gently caressing a sprouting bud hidden beneath the foliage, I breathed, " . . . so tender and so pure."

Bi caught the quiver on my lips.

"What you say?"

I made a half-turn, then leaned down low to stroke its velvet buds. "Oh, nothing, Bi. It isn't important, really."

27
Tragedy in San Diego

Extended Family

N ew Year's Eve, 1982—Hanh's nerves waxed raw from the phone call he received only moments before. He threw his coat on recklessly and raced out the door into the evening air. Jamming his fists deep into his pockets, he increased his pace against the frosty blast. Wandering the side streets of Bryan in a fog, he plowed through the dampness. His feet skimmed over the frozen ground as he ran . . . ran until each step felt like a hammer blow.

The hurt within started like a tiny spot and gradually spread throughout his entire being. He ached all over as his mind throbbed with the heartache of the moment.

"No, no, no!" he repeated time and again, as though the mantra could stamp the dark clouds from his mind.

Suddenly, he stopped short. Tumbling breathless against a lonely lamp post, the twenty-degree temperature froze his inner membranes. His breaths thawed when he exhaled, but froze again when he inhaled into his shivering body.

Why was Hanh running, running, running?

Trying to grapple with his emotions, he swallowed hard. He needed time and space to refigure his future, a future that, until today, had looked hopeful. Chastising himself bitterly, he cursed his inability to grapple with the conundrum.

Hanh's wanton steps began to quicken in the direction of Chung's apartment. Once there, he slumped into a chair and buried his head in his hands. The tears that threatened finally cut loose, and he collapsed emotionally. Hanh wept until his sobbing was coarse and harsh and painful.

◄o►

My mind reeled when Billie called with the news.

"Jeanne," she said, "they think they have to leave. Uncle's been diagnosed with cancer. He's terminal."

"Oh, Billie," I cried, "it can't be true!"

"I'm afraid it is, honey."

She had learned Uncle was having surgery several days before, but only now, was assimilating the repercussions.

"He has cancer of the liver, only three to six months to live."

My eyes squeezed shut, wanting to deny what I was hearing.

The doorbell rang.

"Billie, can I call you later? Someone's here."

We hung up, and I trotted across the room to answer.

My relief was short-lived. There stood Hanh, his head hanging low.

"Mommy call you?" he mumbled.

I peered into his weathered face. "Yes, a few minutes ago she did," I said. "Come in, Hanh. Tell me more about Uncle."

He stepped inside and sank into our maple rocker while I perched on a footstool.

"Uncle call me," he said.

"I know."

"Mommy tell you?"

"She did."

"Uncle dying, Chean. I mus' go him, Calnifornya."

He gazed nervously into the shadows of the hallway.

"But Hanh," I said, confused. "I thought Uncle was angry with you."

"No, Chean. Uncle veddy luf' me. He upset becau' we not lif' wit' him when he go Calnifornya. But now he dying. I mus' go, take care his family."

My mind, still spinning with the news, finally came full circle. In light of Uncle's impending death, Hanh's Asian duty would be to cremate him, and then, to care for Uncle's widow.

Moments later, Herb barged through the door.

"Herb," I said, "did Billie talk to you?"

"Yes, she said Hanh was here, so I came over."

◄o►

Herb underlined our questions for Hanh with cautious sensitivity. "Hanh," he asked, "tell us why you think you must leave."

The lump in Hanh's throat obstructed his ability to speak. When he finally began, he could not hide the sadness in his voice.

"In Vietnam," he said, "if my father die, I mus' go his house, take care my mother, brother, sister."

"But what about your job, Hanh? Must you give it up, too?"

"Everyt'ing. I mus' leave my house, my job, everyt'ing."

"But this is Uncle, not your father," I pleaded.

His eyes searched for answers. "Yeah," he choked, "but in Vietnam, Uncle gif' my family four t'ousand dollah. He safe our life. Nor' Vietnam want kill him becau' he help me. I mus' go Uncle now and help him what I can."

Searching for what to say next, I recalled the $200 Hanh accumulated in his saving since purchasing his car.

"Hanh," I ventured, "Why can't you go to California, just for two or three weeks?"

I pleaded with him to compromise. "You're laid off now from your job, so the timing is good. That way, you can see Uncle before he dies, and then come home to Bi and the children."

"No," he retorted sadly. "Uncle veddy luf' me, Chean. He safe my family. I mus' care his family now."

Hanh's words were sad, but decisive. Decorum determined his destiny. His Asian duty dictated that he take over Uncle's role as the head of the household in his extended family. He must do what he had to do.

Hanh left us, then, and drove straight to Billie's. There, he laid his head in her lap and they wept together, sharing their grief as only a mother and son can do.

◄○►

MiRan perched her soft cheek against my shoulder when I stooped to tell her. Her lip drooped, and then, pouted. Her friends were leaving forever, and she didn't like it one bit.

I, too, wanted to deny what destiny had doled out to Hanh and Bi's family. Torn from their baby and homeland, forced to swim for their lives, and subjected to continuous disparagement from an unforgiving relative whose heart was as hard as the rocks of Malaysia, finally in America they had found peace of mind, a home, and a compassionate church family. And now they were being wrenched from us because of a cruel stroke of fate.

Yet the mind has a way of assuaging our pain. The sand of the desert scorches, but it also polishes. Ice freezes but numbs the pain. The burning sun rakes us through the fire, but it purifies and refines.

And so their loyalties would change—change from our caring church family to their birth family in San Diego. Though our sponsorship was coming to an end, it would forever remain an important chapter in their life journey.

◄o►

We hovered over the map reciting the names of towns like an incantation. I spoke quietly, as a service to my friends, trying to stifle my emotions.

Hanh clenched the tattered edge of the Atlas to steady his trembling hands. "I cannot drive so far," came his tired admission. "I not drive long time Ohio. I t'ink I cannot do."

I looked from Hanh to Bi, who bit her lower lip while glaring at the map. Her bravery saddened me.

"So what is the best way to get there, Hanh?"

"I mus' sell our car 'n' fly Calnifornya," he said.

Bi sat stoically, not daring to express her feelings. Hanh was her husband, and she had to comply.

I folded my hands to think.

"Hanh," I finally said, "if you can wait two more weeks, until the 17th, I'm flying to a conference at the Heifer Ranch in Arkansas. If you can wait, I'll go to Chicago with you. Can you, Hanh?"

"Yeah," he sighed with measured relief.

I slapped my knee. "Good," I exclaimed. "We'll go to Chicago together!"

◄o►

Hanh was right about the car. It would be best to relinquish it. San Diego was 2,000 miles West, across the vast plains of America and over the Rocky Mountains. He wasn't that experienced.

The couple looked sadly at each other, frightened at what awaited them.

Again, Bi started sobbing. "Uncle's wife. She talk, Chean. She talk too much. When we leave Malaysia, I don' want see her again."

She dropped her eyes, resigned. "But now I mus' go my husban'."

I wondered about Bi's feelings. I feared, too, that as the secondary homemaker in an extended family, she would carry the burden.

"Bi," I cried. "Why must you go? Hanh's aunt seems so . . . " I wrenched my mind for a superlative to accentuate her disposition, then settled with, "so insensitive."

Hanh looked at me squarely in the eyes, his demeanor communicating the duty in his. "Chean," he begged, "Uncle is dying. He saf' our life. We mus' care Uncle's wife now. Our God tells us to help her."

172

His countenance dropped. "Maybe some day we can luf' her, too, like Mommy Ame'dica luf' us."

Hanh swallowed hard, and then continued. "When my family come Ame'dica, we worry and we worry. We don' know about sponsor, goot or bad. But you goot to us, so goot. We don' want go Calnifornya, but Uncle sick. He saf' my life, Chean. We mus' go now an' help him before he die."

Bi echoed Hanh's decision in her bleak eyes. I saw her submitting to the husband of her youth from an eternity ago. She was the one I worried for now. But Hanh had spoken and, as his spouse, duty impelled her to accept his wisdom.

—◄◦►—

That night I slid between the blankets. A cold chill tingled down my spine. The covers felt like an air pocket between the frosted ground and a sliver of ice on a frozen puddle. I lay there until the sheets began to warm to the heat of my body.

How could Hanh tell our members, our loyal church people who followed and loved and supported his family, that now they were going to leave?

Someday, I thought, *wherever we live, the doorbell will ring. Our son, Adam, will answer. In will come My and Tuan, no longer frolicking as children, but straining their memories for glimpses of our former lives together. Bi will be older, as will we, our complexions creased with the lines of aging. She'll float into my arms, and we'll weep tears of joy. Hanh will stand proud, no longer a forlorn refugee, but as a citizen of his adopted country. He'll shake Herb's hand vigorously and nod his head in that all too familiar fashion. He may even sport an American mustache, but the old Hanh will still be there, true, stalwart, and loyal, under his Asian exterior.*

—◄◦►—

That Sunday Herb decided that Hanh should share with our members what happened. Perhaps they would understand if it came from him directly. When the appointed time came that morning, Earl assisted Hanh to the microphone.

He began, "I ask Daddy Ame'dica to help me tell you why my family mus' go Calnifornya. In Vietnam, I was farmer. Soldiers come, invade my country. They shoot my dog, steal my crops, take my land. They kill, kill, kill many people. Bi and my family escape.

"My Uncle, in Calnifornya now, he sell everyt'ing he haf' to help me.

173

He pay four t'ousand dollah, my family to go boat. Nort' Vietnam try kill him."

Earl squeezed Hanh's shoulder, then slipped his arm around his waist.

Hanh continued. "In Ame'dica you say family come firs'. Now I mus' go Uncle's house to help him. Maybe then I feel better for what he did for me."

Hanh hung his head. "Uncle veddy sick. He in hospital now. Doctor can not help him. Uncle want me come, lif' wit' him before he die, an' take care his family. About that, we mus' go my Uncle's house. We luf' an' never forget you. You help us in Ame'dica. T'ank you."

Earl had no need for comment. Hanh expressed it well.

—◀○▶—

Herb took the microphone and reflected. "Sometimes, as a church, we're called to reach out to others."

He paused and looked over the sea of faces. Betty was weeping, and so was Paul, as were Blanche and Howard and others around them. The Leslies were doing their best to check their emotions. The whole Killian clan— Grandma Ruby, Marshall and Arveda, Hazel and Eugene, and even Jim—all had tears in their eyes.

Herb continued, " . . . but we are the ones blessed, instead."

He opened his mouth to continue, but his throat constricted. How could he tell Bi and Hanh goodbye?

He gazed at the floor and gathered his thoughts. Finally, he looked up and gave them his final blessing.

"Goodbye, Hanh and Bi. Goodbye, Tuan and My. You must fly on your own now. We pray that your fledgling spirits will not falter in the days ahead. But most of all, we hope the love you experienced in this church will follow you the rest of your lives. Goodbye, dear friends. We'll miss you."

Suddenly, my young, vivacious, arm-around-everybody husband did something he never did in public before.

He wept.

—◀○▶—

After the service, there were many embraces for Hanh, Bi, and the children. An observer from a distance in those final moments could see two sleek figures: Hanh with his hat and corduroy jacket, and Bi in soft olive with her hair smoothed back. Their cheeks were taut and foreheads drawn under the pressure of weighty decisions. Adults they were, obviously aching, no longer in the quagmire of war but in a country that offered them freedom. Their conundrum now was living as free Westerners or as responsible Asians.

No, we didn't understand, nor could we ever. None of us had walked in their shoes or lived through their experiences.

But there we were, a servant church, working with the Nguyens to rebuild their lives, searching with them for their baby, for the Sunshine in the Shadows, and by God's grace, they found her.

—◦—

Bill stated it best. Back in the vestibule, he approached the family and grasped Hanh's hand. He paused for a moment, then, choked, "I respect you, Hanh, for your decision. Uncle sacrificed for your family, and now you must do that for him. Family is very important."

Hanh nodded his head. "T'ank you," he replied gravely.

Bill gripped his hand as if there were more. Repeating the statement with all the weariness of his empathetic heart, he added, "I honor you, Hanh, for your courage."

Hanh hung his head and nodded. Someone understood him.

I turned from my distant perch in the parlor and sank into the sofa. And in my silent soul I cried, out past Hanh and Bi, the stained glass windows, and the sky, and whatever goes past those into the great incredible forever.

Oh, Hanh and Bi, we free you now, because our God tells us to love you.

28
Our "Last Supper"

Four enormous boxes flapped shut, taking on a life of their own. They wobbled across the living room floor amongst several strangely inanimate ones. More than once the spirited packages tipped clumsily on their sides to reveal an entangled mesh of giggling children.

"Hanh, you can't take everything with you!" Billie admonished. "In America men and woman are equal. Bi must take her things, too."

"Mommy, I want take this, 'n' this," Hanh wailed, attempting to wile her to his way of thinking.

Billie intercepted and gave Bi permission to pack several pots and pans, plus her wardrobe and a few perfumes and powders.

I swallowed a laugh as Bi slipped a sachet into the cavity of a vaporizer. Another she plucked from the pile and threw into the waste basket. Hanh retrieved it and tucked it into her luggage. Bi removed it. Hanh put it back again.

"No, no!" Bi protested. This time she saw me watching. A foolish grin cowered across her face. "Hanh like this. I don'," she said.

I reached for the tiny cache. It smelled like rancid strawberry.

Hanh retreated into his shell, resigned to being outnumbered. He couldn't argue with Chean in the room. Bi glanced askance at us, then grinned to herself and confidently dropped the bottle into the trash again.

Another small victory for the little Asian woman!

◄o►

That weekend, Bob and Verle backed their truck up to the Nugyens' apartment. One room at a time, they emptied the home of all traces of their existence. Hanh moved in a trance-like state from one memory-laden room to another, walls echoing our footsteps like ghosts in haunted enclaves. The silence was distressing.

Though Bi's eyes mirrored a dreadful void, the children scampered through the rooms as though finality were not an issue. Suddenly in a single, boorish moment, the telephone jangled, oblivious to our sensibilities.

"Hello," Hanh sighed, in English. His language soon metamorphosed into intonations of Vietnamese. Bi listened intently to the conversation.

Hanh clicked the receiver down in a lighter frame of mind. "You know, Chean, I tell you I haf' cousin, she marry Ame'dican husban' eight year ago?"

I strained my mind for the memory.

"I don' know where cousin lif', but she call me now. My friend write her. He tell her I lif' Bryan."

"Where is she, Hanh?"

"Indiyana, she say."

"Indiana! Oh, Hanh, we could have visited her! We're only twenty miles from the border!"

He cocked his head in my direction. "What you say?"

I tried to curb their disappointment by restraining my voice. "If you weren't leaving for California, we could go and visit her."

On second thought, I added, "Hanh, you can still change your mind, and stay here, I mean. Your furniture's at the church, and your rent is good until Monday."

Hanh looked at me, wistfully. His primitive emotions wanted to comply, but instead, he dropped his head, resigned to his Asian duty.

"Chean, I mus' go Uncle now. I mus' go before he die."

—◄o►—

That Sunday the church honored the family with a voluminous potluck and a keepsake album of memories. The following week, Bi and Hanh cooked dinner for those of us who worked with them on a daily basis.

Aromas of ginger root and sesame oil saturated the house that evening. As Earl ushered us into the living room, we felt like honored guests at an extravagant restaurant. Sniffing the aromatic spices, we floated into the kitchen where Bi and Hanh were tossing together an exotic concoction.

I glanced across the room. Mabel, Florence, and Wilma, their English teachers were there—those whose faithfulness over many months enabled the family to move from "Chau' to nouns, verbs and linguistic constructions. Mary and Blaine, who gave them a gift certificate for use in an Asian grocery store, were present to share their culinary prowess. And Jerry and Sharon with her contagious laughter joined our entourage for the evening.

Adam and MiRan disappeared into the playroom to piece together

Hanh in background as Mother Bi dishes out *Mao Sai*
for the pastor's children, Adam and MiRan.

puzzles with My and Tuan. Stealthily, they closed the door to conceal their mischievous antics.

Herb and I sank into cushions on the sofa, sensing the absence of someone special.

"Paul and Betty can't make it tonight," Billie said. "Paul's been so helpful, and Betty faithfully took Bi for groceries every week. We really depended on her."

We were disappointed that Paul and Betty couldn't be with us. Their gracious spirits brought joy to all they encountered, and they had helped to lighten the church's financial burdens more times than we could number.

Arranging the family's flights with mine as far as Chicago was no problem.

"Tomorrow will be busy," I told Billie. "To be honest, though, I'm glad I have to pack. It'll keep me busy."

Mary chimed in. "I wish I could check my feelings in with yours."

We joined hands in prayer around the table for our last meal together. Sadness filled the air as Herb provided the grace. Hanging onto every word, his prayer extolled our human connection, our extended hands linking in a circle of love together.

Bi uncovered each dish with a dramatic flourish, and their apartment took on the ambiance of an Asian festival. We savored morsels of pork roll, *me sau*, and other Vietnamese delicacies: pinches of dough steamed with sausage and eggs, and spicy soup slurped from blue lotus bowls. Chopsticks dipped sticky rice balls into one condiment after another.

The mood was light, and trying to be cheerful finally metamorphosed into the real thing. From time to time, flashbulbs carved tender moments out of an evening to be remembered. An event of beautiful memories was etching itself in history.

Soon, time had a way of swallowing up the hours, and we all disappeared into the night.

─◄o►─

In the week that followed, we talked with Hanh about the car. He knew he couldn't drive it all the way to California.

After work one night, he slipped out of their apartment and sat behind the wheel of his Buick. Soon, the sun crested, arching its way toward the western sky. He stroked his hand over the rich, leathery dashboard that he and Earl had meticulously scrubbed the evening before, in hopes of getting a better price.

Hanh flicked the key and let the engine hum, its pulsations soothing the tumult in his mind. This car had been his passage to freedom, his ticket to independence. But now he had to sell it to buy another ticket, and to exchange his freedom for loyalty to family.

Grasping the keys, he flicked off the ignition. As a man, he had lived through all he could handle these past few years. Yet honor compelled him to take one more step to perform his Asian duty. It would require all the strength he could muster.

Frustrated at his lack of courage, he swallowed the lump in his throat, then swung his legs to the left and thrust his body out of the car. Straightening his back, he smoothed his rumpled jacket and jerked his head upward to catch the Ohio wind.

Shutting the door behind him, he took a series of slow, measured steps into the house and handed the keys to Daddy America.

◄○►

Bi crumpled to the floor and laid her head in Earl's lap. "I don' want leave my Daddy," she sobbed, "but Hanh is my husban' an' we mus' go."

Daddy America stroked her black, sleek hair. These last few hours together were achingly precious, but heartrending.

Billie blinked back tears, trying her best to lighten the mood. "Hanh," she asked, "can you sing for us the song you sang at the lake?"

Hanh stammered, "No, Mommy, I cannot do."

"Please," Billie persisted. "Just a little song for me? I'll record it so I can remember you."

"I cannot sing tonight, Mommy."

Billie's blue eyes filled with tenderness. Then, ignoring the tenor of the moment, she scooped Tuan up off the floor and tickled his paunchy belly.

"Gramma, Gramma!" he giggled.

Grandma perched him on her knee while My cuddled nearby. The children heard they were going somewhere, but emotionally the news meant little.

Tuan rolled his eyes in Billie's direction, "Gramma," he said, "when Tuan get big, he get wife, two boys, one girl. We come your house."

Stunned by his childish pronouncement, Billie smiled. "How will you 'come my house', Tuan?" she asked.

"In big car," he answered, stretching his arms to illustrate.

"You mean little car?" Earl teased.

"No, big car—so Gramma can fit!" he retorted.

A shudder of comic relief shook Billie's body, and she began to chuckle. The merriment became contagious, and shortly, all were laughing.

"Tuan," Billie asked, "will you say that again, just for Grandma, on the recorder?"

"Yeah," his dark eyes answered. "I come big car so Gramma can fit!"

My's perky demeanor vied for Grandma's attention. "My come, too?" she asked.

"Sure," Billie smiled, deferring to her enthusiasm.

Earl placed his recorder in the middle of the table to catch the innocent chatter of two far-away children very much present in the moment.

Hanh crossed the carpeted room and quietly sat at Billie's feet. In a quivering voice, he began to sing songs of long ago and far away—songs of Tet, the Chinese New Year, and new beginnings for his family.

Soon his words trailed off, but not until Billie recorded son number three's last gift for his American parents. The hush that followed was laden with emotion.

Silence did the speaking for them.

Earl broke the quiescence for them.

"Hanh," he said, "when the time comes for you to get your baby, call us, and we will help you."

Bi looked up, alive with attention.

Hanh cleared his throat. "You help us in Calnifornya?"

"Yes. We talked to Wilma. She wrote to our church in San Diego. Their ministers are friends of hers. They were on the mission field together in Nigeria."

Bi sat quietly, assimilating each word. "Wilma know them?"

"Yes," Earl continued. "Their names are Irven and Patty Stern."

"When the papers arrive," Billie explained, "we will send them to you. Then you can apply for your baby. Irven and Patty said they'll help you with the forms, too."

The scimitar curve of Bi's high cheekbones caught the glow of the lamplight. "Church people in Calnifornya are goot . . . like you?"

"They're good, honey. You'll like them."

A flicker of light crossed Bi's countenance. The couple glanced at each other, relieved.

Earl regarded his adoptive children with a secret sadness that ran through him like pangs of hunger. "You must pray every night," he said, "that God will bring your baby home to you."

Leaning back in his chair, Earl knew Hanh well enough to read his emotions. He thought to himself, *Hanh and Bi, as a couple, the two of you have survived a war. With God's grace, you can survive the shadows. Our prayer for you now is that you can reclaim the sunshine.*

With that, he relinquished his Asian family to the future and prayed that he and Billie had taught them all they needed to survive. Earl's role as "daddy" was finished.

29

Break the Bread of Life with Us

Grace and Hope for the Future

"Goodbye, Snoopy!" I called, as Adam shuffled out the door lugging his school bag behind him. As an afterthought, I added, "See you Sunday, honey!"

"Bye, Mom! Love ya'!" he retorted.

Staggering a row of footprints behind him in the thinly crested snow, I watched my son of eight years get swallowed by the yellow monster that scuttled him up the road toward the schoolhouse. Rolling a few more feet, it stopped again amidst blinking lights to swallow up yet another household of children.

After I closed the door behind me, MiRan bounded down the steps with sleep still in her eyes. After a habitual swallow of milk, she came alive.

"You'll take care of Daddy, won't you?"

She blinked and then remembered. Today was Mommy's day to leave.

"Yeah," she yawned. "Is *Captain* on?"[20]

I flicked the TV to her favorite program, but kept the volume low.

"MiRan, I'll be with you this morning, but this afternoon Dad will take you to Norma's."

She exuded a sigh of relief. She loved to play in Norma's craft room. It was laden with bangles and beads.

In the busy hours that transpired, the ticking clock cut the morning into slices. When Herb returned for lunch, my time had come to leave.

Bidding them farewell, I hypnotically navigated our old green Dodge across the city of Bryan.

As I glided to a halt in front of Nugyens' apartment, curtains brushed aside, rumpling at the sill. Four little eyes peered out at me, the scene familiar down to the lurid details.

Captain Kangaroo was a favorite television program of children in the 1970s.

I entered their abode, strangely silent now. Billie was there to bid the family farewell. The anguished expression on her face gave way to her inner emotions. She had promised Bi she wouldn't cry, at least not until they left, but the strain of the moment was more than she could handle.

Hanh nervously twitched his hands, withdrawn from conversation. The pink in Bi's suit accentuated her cheeks, pale from weakened courage. Crescents of flesh under her swollen eyes revealed how she spent the previous night.

Billie slid two small coats over the children's shoulders. Then, wrapping them in her arms, she peppered them with kisses.

When she turned to Bi to bid her farewell, Bi hugged her hard and ranted, "Mommy, Mommy, Mommy!"

Billie's arms were full of Bi, her coal black hair, her thin frail body, crying out to save her, but the heartbroken Bi clung to Billie and refused to release her.

I felt the blood coursing through my veins. Closing my eyes, I silently cried, 'God, grant them mercy, just a gossamer thread of assurance that You will be there for them.'

"Mommy! Mommy!" Bi wailed, clutching Billie with all the strength inside her.

Billie gently nudged her. "You must go now, Bi. Jeanne is waiting for you."

Bi swallowed her unwelcome tears, lowering her countenance to hide them.

When Billie reached for Hanh, he stiffened his back and buried his head on her shoulder. Taking one last look at Mommy America, he snapped her image permanently in his mind, then stepped into my car ready to face an unknown future.

—◄o►—

We did not converse as the Studebaker swept us through landmarks on the map—Bryan, West Unity, and Delta—retracing the path that brought them to us nine months prior. Hanh pursed his lips in stoic manner while Bi, who sat in front beside me, peered out the window to conceal her sobbing.

Only a few months prior, this family had fled a war and traveled halfway around the span of the globe to find a semblance of freedom. Their heartache was immeasurable, their loss almost unfathomable, but I knew in my heart that their spirits were resilient and they would thrive again.

—◄o►—

Tuan and My wave goodbye at the Toledo airport.

Tripping through the turnstile with their luggage, the hum of their plane droned in the background as we boarded. An hour later, the rush of the jet thrust us over Toledo, our long, gray Leviathan soaring gracefully above the clouds intercepting the earth below us.

Bi leaned toward me. "Chean?"

She spoke with hushed inflection. "Las' night Hanh tell Mommy 'n' Daddy that maybe we come Ohio when Uncle die. He say to Mommy, Chean!" Her eyes were alight with hope.

Tuan tugged at my arm from his window seat. He needed attention, too.

"What does our little panda want?" I retorted.

"We go airplane," he said. "We get Ngoc My. We haf" two babies now!"

I looked to Bi for an explanation.

Smiling sadly, she said, "Tuan t'ink we go airplane, get baby. He don' listen about Uncle . . . about why we go Calnifornya. He say we get two baby now, Tuan and Ngoc My."

Tuan's innocent fantasies filled the silence. My heart wanted to weep, but it forced a smile, instead.

◄○►

An hour later, we circled the haze over Chicago and our jet descended slowly into O'Hare. Hovering over Lake Michigan, the breaking waves offered up a wreath that stung like tears below us.

Inside the terminal, a dozen times we read a dozen different schedules on the marquis above us. Pointing toward a silver message on the screen, I read, "Flight 419! Hanh, do you see it? At 6:03 you will leave at Gate 23."

Tracing the iridescent numbers with his finger in the air, he said, "Yeah. This I mus' remember."

My clamored to her mother's side. "My hungwy, Mommy, Tuan 'n' me."

Bi glanced at me. "We get somet'ing for children, Chean?"

We set out alone, leaving Hanh to watch the little ones. Weaving through crowds of travelers and business stalls, planes poured their human cargo, one passenger after another, into the wavering concourse.

Suddenly, Bi spied an empty niche where we ran for cover. I sank into a settee, and she settled in beside me. Together, we laughed like teenagers, giggling at our shenanigans.

Bi tossed her head back and discovered a cactus cascading over her shoulder. Weighted down in blossom, in a moment of reprieve, she plucked a bloom and presented it to me.

"Heah, Chean," she said. "Take this. You my sister now."

She offered the bloom again.

I accepted it and noticed its winey color and broken stem. A drop of life-giving sap seeped from its wound. Severed from its source of nourishment, its demise was certain, yet I knew in my heart that the bud would blossom again.

—◦—

We found the food court, returned to the gate, and searched for ways to slow the time. The afternoon sun beamed through the windows, sculpting us into shadows. Checking my watch methodically, finally I had to leave.

The words forced themselves from my throat. "It's almost 5:00. I must catch my plane to Toledo now."

My looked at me when I stooped down to hug her.

"You go now, Chean?"

I nodded.

"G'bye," she waved.

"Bye, honey," I choked, and kissed her golden forehead.

Trying my best to check emotions, I reached for Tuan, skipped the goodbye, then hugged him. Somehow, it seemed too final.

Turning toward Bi, our arms encircled each other. She was beautiful when she cried, but so sad.

Extending my hand to Hanh, he swallowed hard.

"We don' say so much now, Chean."

"Thanks," I said, grateful for his sensitivity.

Bi dug in her pocket for a package of tissues. I glanced at her for a fleeting moment, her cheeks, flushed and red. "Mommy gif' me," she mumbled. A moment of forlorn laughter passed between us.

"Bi," I rasped. "We're acting like a funeral!"

She darted a glance askance at me, her tears swallowing our laughter.

Taking one last glance at the beautiful family that flitted into and out of our lives like a fragment of a dream, I thanked the Mighty God that we were privileged to share a chapter with them.

Threading my way through the terminal and the strange, uncaring faces, around the corner and out of sight, the tears streamed freely. I let them flow. They did not bother me, for sorrow is the deepest emotion, and I would, and could not hide it.

During our year together, we searched with Bi and Hanh for the sunshine in the shadows, and by God's grace, we found it.

Epilogue

For Hope and Peace

◄○►

Resettling the Nguyen family after the Vietnam War was one of the most powerful experiences in the life of our church. During the year we resettled the family, we lived their story with them. Their journey is not one we would have chosen for ourselves, no, not in a thousand years, but had we not shared in their agony, we would surely have missed the ecstasy.

◄○►

In 2015, thirty-five years after Bi and Hanh left us, Herb and I stopped in Vietnam on our way home from India. To our surprise, the country was celebrating Tet, the Chinese New Year.

Rick-shawing our way to the parade that day, horns honked incessantly. Vendors crowded the streets, their rickety storefronts overflowing with merchandise. Parents paraded their children through the crowds while peddlers hawked their wares. Donkeys lumbered along in traffic, farm carts in tow, a wonderful madhouse of bedlam—succulently delightful!

Though the city was teaming with humanity, their families appeared content, living their lives oblivious to the war as though it never happened. Today's toddlers, great-grandchildren of the war's survivors, were dressed to the hilt for Children's Day, a symbol of hope for their tomorrows. The pain of past years seemed but a fragment of history.

Yes, life goes on for today's generation, the past a remnant of old people's dreams. The Vietnam War of bygone years seemed buried in the past, forgotten by the country's children. During Tet 2015, the pain and sorrow seemed to have vanished, darkness giving way to new tomorrows.

Watching the elderly hobble through crowds, many appeared withered, withdrawn, their lives the fallout of yesteryear. In the midst of traffic and blaring horns, I wondered how they survived the horrors. I wondered, too, about their stories—the trauma, the terror, the crossfire, destruction, and blood shed by loved ones in their families.

187

A pacifist by birth and by faith, I harbored with them the hurt in their hearts. Forty years after the war's demise, only time could assuage the pain of their past. Thus, I sorrowed for them—and for all of us.

Yet today was a day of celebration. Though the elderly, wrinkled and drawn, with scars of suffering embedded in their memories, their children and grandchildren wandered the streets in the ambiance of peace.

◄o►

The Nguyens in their new home in San Diego, California: Bi and Hanh, Tuan and My

Back in the states, I dialed Hanh and Bi in San Diego. Bi was excited to tell me that she is now the proud proprietor of her own manicure salon. Hanh worked until recently, but he is now retired.

Upon naturalization, My and Tuan took on new identities. My adopted the American name, 'Kim', and earned her doctorate in pharmacy. Tuan, now naturalized as 'David', is a Certified Public Accountant. Both are living worthy lives in their adopted country.

Fourteen years after the war's end, the Nguyens were finally reunited with Ngoc My. To avoid trauma during her infancy, they decided, in concert with Hanh's parents, to leave the child in Vietnam until she could make the 8,000 mile journey. Today, Ngoc My is a bona-fide American citizen, naturalized as 'Amy'.

After 14 years of heartbreak and separation, the Nguyens, at last, reclaimed their missing daughter. Today, they live with Amy and her family in an extended household together.

◄o►

The Nguyens' experience during the Indochina War is not one they would have chosen for their lives—no, not in a thousand years. Yet conflict happens and innocents suffer the fallout of war's collateral.

Because Church World Service and its resettlement staff was on the ground when the fighting drew to a close, the agency assessed the family's needs, and found them a home in a receiving country. After their arrival in the United States, the organization's compassionate ministry kept track of them and reunited their family.

That year of reprieve in Ohio when our church resettled them now seems but an episode in history, yet for the family, it was a time of healing. The cadence in Bi's voice across the miles communicated that to me.

Such is the hallmark of sponsorship: To rescue the lost and the homeless, to walk them through their new culture, to be there when they need us, and then, to set them free.

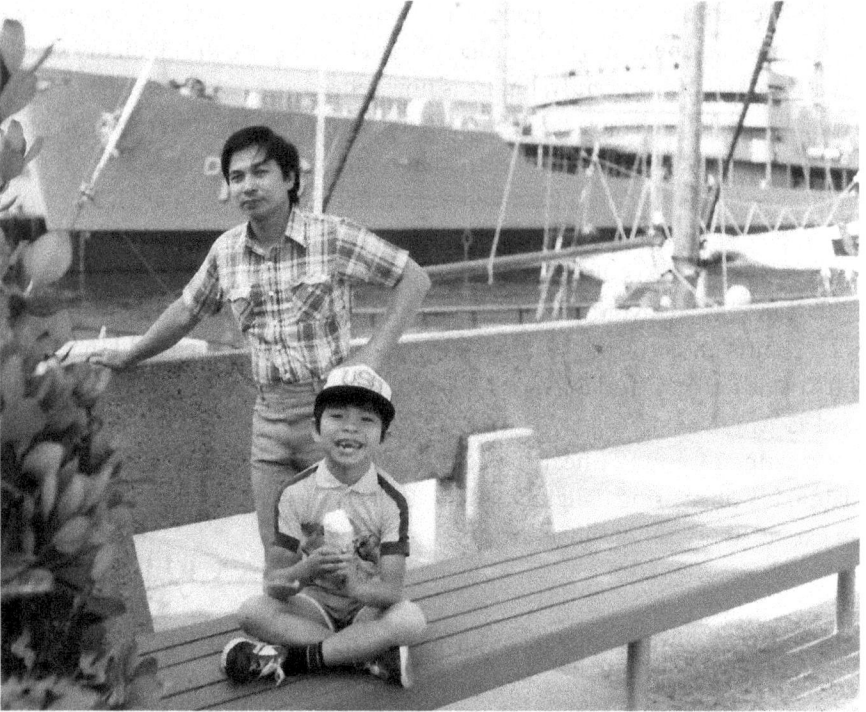

Photo Credit: Myrna Grove

Hanh and Tuan in a San Diego shipyard, six months after they left Bryan, Ohio.

Tuan and My in San Diego

Hanh and Bi Nguyen, at left, returned to Bryan, Ohio, to visit Billie (center) in recent years. They met Chan and Van Phomsavanh, (at right) from Burma, the second refugee family resettled by the church.

Hanh and Bi Nguyen visiting Bryan, Ohio, May 2008

Bi and Hanh Nguyen with Billie Kornrumpf, whom they called "Mommy Ame'dica" and who helped them resettle in Bryan, Ohio

Tuan "David" Nguyen works as a C.P.A. May 2008

My, naturalized as "Kim," is a lead pharmacist in San Diego. Her two sons are with her, May, 2008

Guidelines for Groups Resettling Refugees Today

To escape conflict and persecution, more people than ever before have fled their homes and become refugees. Many agencies and organizations work to resettle this unprecedented outpouring of humanity, but cannot solve the global crisis alone. Refugees need homes and communities to settle in, with the welcoming support of sponsors who care about them.

FIRST STEPS

The first thing your sponsoring group or congregation will need to do is to set up a meeting to determine the interest of members in undertaking the project of sponsoring refugees. Then contact one of the agencies in the following list to match you up with a refugee family and make arrangements for their travel. The agency will help you tailor your expectations and set the goal of your project, i.e. length of support.

Ask for volunteers and set up a resettlement committee with subcommittees to take care of tasks in each category listed below. Some tasks will need to be completed before your refugees arrive.

PRE-ARRIVAL PROCESSES

1. **Legal Issues** – U.S. Citizenship and Immigration Services (USCIS) in the Department of Homeland Security will conduct interviews with your refugee(s) abroad to determine their eligibility for "refugee status" in the United States. Check with your church's sponsoring agency (i.e., Church World Service, Episcopalian, Mennonite Relief, Catholic, etc.) regarding paperwork that must be completed before and/or after their arrival. Care for this in a timely manner before their arrival.

2. **Refugee Travel Loans** – These promissory notes (loans) are issued to refugees 18 yeas of age and older prior to their arrival in the U.S. Provided by the International Organization for Migration, they cover costs of refugees' transport from point of origin to their resettlement destination. Medical screening is included in the fee. This legal document confirms

the refugees' willingness to repay the loan in monthly installments. The loan is interest-free and is administered by the U.S. State Department's Bureau for Population. Refugees must begin payments no later than six months after their arrival. Repayment funds will be used by the U.S. government to assist future refugees.

For further information, speak with an agent at your denomination's refugee resettlement office. (See resettlement agencies' contact information at the end of this book). Also, for any updates or changes, check this website: www.ssa.gov

3. **Health Issues and Immunizations (pre-arrival)** – All refugees are required to have a thorough physical exam before coming to the United States. This includes screening for malaria and intestinal parasites before leaving the country of origin. Children must have proper inoculations before enrolling in school. See "Guidelines for the U.S. Domestic Medical Examination for Newly Arriving Refugees." Website: http:www.cdc. gov/immigrantrefugeehealth/guidelines/refugee-guidelines.html.

COMMITTEES AND TASKS

WELCOMING COMMITTEE

A small group from your church should go to the airport to welcome your refugee(s). This may include your pastor, member(s) of your Resettlement Committee, your host family, and others, as desired. Introduce yourselves to them to put them at ease. Take jackets, coats, hats, umbrellas, etc. in the event they arrive without proper attire for the climate. **websites for welcoming refugees***
www.cwsglobal.org/our-work/refugee-services/welcoming-refugees.html
www.cwsglobal.org/get-involved/welcome-a-refugee

Note: Host Family – If your refugees' initial, temporary housing is arranged with a host family, they will become acclimated to the American way of life more quickly.

HOUSING AND FURNISHINGS COMMITTEE

Apartment Setup/Donations Drive – Hold a Donations Drive to collect furniture and amenities for your refugees' apartment. If household items are used, they should be clean and in good condition.

Typical items:

a. Cleaning supplies – broom, dustpan, mop, bucket, furniture polish, laundry basket(s) and detergent, clothes pins, washline (rope), vacuum cleaner, cleansers and cloths, etc.

b. Living Room – sofa, easy chair, end table, lamps, a telephone (landline), an area set aside for studying English (a table or desk), paper and pencils, dictionary, books, television (optional), throw rugs, curtains, etc.

c. Kitchen – stove, table and chairs, refrigerator, dishpan, dish-washing liquid, dish cloths, scouring pad, plates, bowls, cups, glasses, silverware, pots and pans, knives, cutting board, spatulas, mixing bowl, hand mixer, water pitcher, can opener (hand operated), tea towels, dishcloths, pot holders, etc.

e. Bedrooms – beds with mattresses, mattress pads, blankets, sheets, pillows, pillow cases, bureau, lamp, clothes hamper and hangers, alarm clock, etc.

f. Bathroom – Shower curtain, bath towels, hand towels, washcloths, soap, tooth brushes, tooth paste, non-electric razors, combs, toilet tissue, shampoo, hair conditioner, first aid kit, sanitary items, floor rug, plunger, toilet cleaning brush, etc.

g. Telephone – Arrange for a landline to be installed in their apartment. Because landlines are tied to specific addresses, if your refugees need to dial 911, the language barrier will not be an issue, as emergency personnel can trace their exact location. Also, write phone numbers in the back of their phone book for the following: their host family, your pastor, their English teachers, driving teacher, the doctor, etc.

h. Other Household Items – flashlight, batteries, umbrella(s), iron, ironing board, snow shovel, and fan, (depending on climate).

When your refugees arrive, teach them how to use electric appliances. Also, show them where the main breaker switch is and how to operate it.

LANGUAGE, EDUCATION, AND CHILDCARE COMMITTEE

Provide English lessons for both parents and children. Some children may learn the language faster than their parents. On the other hand, trauma from recent events in their lives may hold them back. When enrolling your refugees' children in school, go with them to assure they are appropriately enrolled in English as a Second Language classes.

Provide a local phone book, two-way language dictionary, Bible, etc.

English Classes for Adults –

Option A: Many school systems and/or communities offer English as a Second Language (ESL or ESOL) classes for adults during evenings or weekends. Inquire at your local school district and/or your public library about availability. The Department of Education in Washington, DC, administers programs for non-English speakers. A fee may be required.

Option B: Some programs have trained volunteers who serve as tutors for teaching English as a second language. Three options are listed below. Check with your local schools and other resettlement agencies for programs in your area (Episcopalians, Mennonite Relief, Catholic Charities, etc.).

a. Proliteracy – Tutor Training for Teaching Adults
Website: www.proliteracyednet.org/articles.asp?mcid=2&cid=26.
Phone: (888) 528-2224

b. *English-as-a-Second Language Tutor Training Manual: A Learner-Centered Approach to Tutoring Adult ESL Learners*
Website: www.proliteracyednet.org/downloads/73ESLTutorTrainingKit.pdf

c. Pimsleur - English as a Second Language Program
Website: offers.pimsleur.com/Special_Offer003?&utm_source=google&utm_term=+pimsleur%2+programs&utm_campaign=G_Pim_Brand_Plus_BMM&utm_medium=cpc&gclid=CNz9vaH6hcsCFQQEaQodPEcMtw

English as a Second Language for School-age Children – Before your refugees arrive, talk with the principal or counselor in your local school district about providing classes in English as a Second Language for your refugees' children. Work with the teachers and become an advocate for the children.

School-Age Children – On the first day of school, accompany the child and his or her parent to school to meet the teacher and classmates. Arrange for tutors in your sponsoring group or congregation to help them with their homework.

Stay in touch with your refugees' children as they adjust to school. Some may experience prejudice and/or ostracism because they are perceived as 'different'. If there are racial or other problems, talk with their principal and teachers about it. Ask teachers to discuss equity and racism openly in their classrooms without singling out students for being different. Goal: To extol persons of every color, ethnicity, creed, race, religion, and those who feel excluded from the mainstream as worthy human beings in a democratic society.

Pre-school Children –
Refugee children have been traumatized. Thus, most will need time to adjust to their new environment. Encourage their parents to keep the child nearby until he or she is psychologically stable. Later, child care with a sensitive caretaker may be utilized.

Provide simple, basic toys such as dolls, teddy bears, building toys, matchbook cars, balls, jump rope, coloring books, crayons, story books with pictures, etc. Avoid choking items for young children.

MEDICAL COMMITTEE
Health Issues/Immunizations – Refugees are required to have a thorough physical exam before coming to the United States. This includes screening for malaria and intestinal parasites before leaving their country of origin. Children must have appropriate inoculations before enrolling in school. See "Guidelines for the U.S. Domestic Medical Examination for Newly Arriving Refugees" at this website: www.cdc.gov/immigrantrefugeehealth/guidelines/refugee-guidelines.html

Physician/Dentist/ Insurance – After your refugees arrive, check with Church World Service and your local physicians regarding payment options for refugees. An examination is particularly important for mothers who recently gave birth.

CLOTHING COMMITTEE
Most refugees arrive with only the clothing on their backs. If they arrive during winter months, take coats, scarves, hats, gloves, boots, etc., to the airport for their arrival. Put an announcement with a list of needed

items in your church bulletins and newsletter. New and used clothing, if washed and in good condition, are acceptable. Account for seasonal changes.

Note: Clothing should be conservative in style. Parishioners may donate needed items. Check thrift shops for items not given. Wash and iron clothing before delivery.

Women and girls – modest dresses, skirts, blouses, slacks, nightgown/pajamas, slips, underwear, stockings, socks, sweaters, coats/jackets (for spring and winter), warm hat, scarf, shoes, boots, gloves, sanitary products, (depending on age) etc.

Men and boys – shirts, T-shirts, jeans, work pants, trousers, sweaters, pajamas, underwear, jacket, winter coat, warm hat, gloves, boots, shoes, socks, scarf, wallet, etc.

Infants – disposable diapers, or cloth diapers and pins, undershirts, sleepers, milk bottles, formula, pacifier, baby dish and spoon, baby food, bibs, portable bed, bed sheets, receiving blankets, warm blanket, detergent, etc.

Laundry – Show your refugees the nearest laundromat. Demonstrate how to put soap powder into the machines and money into the slots. Needed: detergent, wash baskets, and money for machines. A clothes-drying rack would be helpful to have at home for items that shouldn't be put in a dryer.

FOOD COMMITTEE
Groceries – Show your refugees where the nearest grocery store is located. Draw them a map so they can find it from their apartment.

Stock basic foods in their cupboards and refrigerator just before their arrival – meat (unless they are vegetarians), fruits, vegetables, canned beans, soup, rice, bread, butter, salt and pepper, sugar, cooking oil, flour, eggs, cereal, peanut butter, jam, milk, juice, etc.

Become familiar with your refugees' ethnic cuisine. After their arrival, give them a tour of the local grocery store. Show them where to find basic foods and the ethnic food section. Help them to make healthy food choices. Give them a pocket-sized calculator to keep track of their spending.

EMPLOYMENT COMMITTEE

Social Security and Green Card – Refugees must have a Green Card to work legally in the United States. A Social Security number is required before one can apply for the Green Card. To apply for Social Security, call 1-800-772-1213.

Procedure: (1) Complete Form SS-5 and send in the application for Social Security. (2) After your Social Security card arrives, use Form I-485 to apply for a Green Card (Application to Register for Permanent Residence or Adjust Status). Check this government website for any updates or changes: www.ssa.gov

Members of your sponsoring group or your church should work with your refugees to help them find employment. Check with your resettlement agency regarding requirements and procedures. Website: www.uscis.gov/green-card/green-card-through-refugee-or-asylee-status/green-card-refugee

TRANSPORTATION COMMITTEE

After your refugees arrive, arrange for their transport to church, work, school, the grocery store, doctor, etc. Take them on a driving tour of your community to familiarize them with key locations.

Provide a map of your town with landmarks circled, i.e., their apartment, host family, place of employment, grocery store, the children's school, your church, the pastor's residence, doctor's office, location of English lessons, a park, and other important locations.

Driving lessons & license – Getting a license is a major accomplishment for refugees, as it signals their independence. As your refugees become more fluent in English, the head of the household may begin studying for a driver's license. Ask for a volunteer to help interpret the driver's manual. Provide driving lessons. When you are confident the refugees are ready, go with them to apply for their driver's license. Remind them to take their Green Card and any other evidence that they are legally in the country on the day of their driving test. Check with local authorities regarding necessary paperwork, as some states differ in their requirements.

Purchase of a Car – Until they receive or purchase a car, you will need to arrange for their transport to jobs, the grocery store, English lessons, the doctor, church, etc. Check local sources for used cars or individuals willing to donate a vehicle. When your refugees do get a car, show them how to buy gasoline and make sure they understand basic auto care and maintenance.

FINANCES AND LEGAL ISSUES COMMITTEE

Budgeting, Banking, Paying Bills – After a job has been secured for the head of the household, help them set up a budget. Go with them to establish a bank account in their name(s). This is essential, as the U.S. government now requires refugees to set up a bank account to pay back their cost of transportation to the country of asylum. (See 'Refugee Travel Loans' above). It is of utmost importance that your refugees honor this obligation. Ensure that they budget a portion of their paycheck for this loan. Show them how to pay telephone, rent, and utility bills. Emphasize the importance of paying bills on time.

Legal Issues/Naturalization – Check with the agency through which you received your refugees (Church World Service, Mennonite Relief, Catholic Charities, etc.) to see what official documents/paperwork needs to be completed before and after the refugees' arrival. See: "Path to Citizenship" guidelines at https://www.uscis.gov/us-citizenship/ citizenship-through-naturalization/path-us-citizenship

SUPPORT SYSTEM

Your members can provide a much-needed support system for your refugees. Invite them to your church gatherings, formal and informal. Visit them regularly. Learn to know each other and appreciate each other's faiths. Help them build relationships. Stay attuned to their needs and help them. Most importantly, befriend them.

Contacts, Phone Numbers, Map, etc. – List phone numbers in the back of their phone book to call in case of emergency. Examples: their host family, your pastor, a deacon, the church, 911, the fire company, the doctor, etc.) Provide your refugees a map of your hometown. Maps may be available at your local Chamber of Commerce.

Visit your refugees frequently to see that their needs are met. Build trust and friendships with them. Invite and transport them to social gatherings. Help them build relationships and integrate into the community. Examples: Sunday services and/or social gatherings, music programs, festivals, potlucks, picnics, ball games, etc. Respect their faith backgrounds. They have lost much already, so do not pressure them to abandon their cultural identity. They will know you are Christians by your love.

PUBLIC RELATIONS COMMITTEE

Update your congregation on your refugees' resettlement progress from time to time. When your refugee(s) find a job or pass their driver's exam, or if special events have occurred in their lives, share them with your congregation.

As needs arise, ask your sponsoring-group members for help. Examples: Moving them into their apartment, providing seasonal clothing for the family, donations of household items/ furnishings, teaching the head of the household to drive, etc. The more involved your congregation is, the more meaningful the resettlement for all. (Website: https://oca.org/parish-ministry/commservice/helping-to-resettle-refugees).

―◁○▷―

REFUGEE RESETTLEMENT AGENCIES

The resettlement process takes commitment, but when a dedicated group of people join together to make it happen, it can become a tremendously gratifying experience. Check with your resettlement agency for details regarding your responsibilities and how to proceed. They will have guidelines to share with you.

Please note: Occasionally, organizations revise their data and a web link becomes non-functional. If this occurs, please Google the organization for their updated information.

CHURCH WORLD SERVICE –

Church World Service (CWS) is a cooperative ministry of 37 Christian denominations and communions affiliated with the National Council of Churches in the United States. It provides sustainable self-help, development, disaster relief, and refugee assistance around the world.
CWS website – www.cwsglobal.org/our-work/refugee-services/welcoming-refugees.html

Church World Service Refugee Resettlement: www.cwsglobal.org/what-we-do/refugees/us-programs/refugee-resettlement.html

CWS Offices in the United States —

Church World Service Immigration and Refugee Program Central Office
475 Riverside Dr., Suite 700, New York, NY 10115
Phone: 212-870-2061; Fax: 212-870-3194 or 212-870-3220
Email: irp@churchworldservice.org
Website: www.supportimmigrationreform.org

Church World Service Advocacy and Policy Office
110 Maryland Ave., N. E., Suite 404
Washington, DC 20002
Phone: 202-481-6936; Fax: 202-546-6232

Church World Service, Elkhart, Indiana
28606 Phillips St., P.O. Box 968
Elkhart, IN 46515
Phone: 800-297-1516 or 574-264-3102; Fax: (574) 262-0966

Church World Service, Harrisonburg, Virginia (regional office)
250 E. Elizabeth St., Suite 109, Harrisonburg, VA 22802
Phone: (540) 433-7942
Website: http://harrisonburgrefugees.com

Church World Service, Lancaster, Pennsylvania – Lancaster County
Refugee Coalition. Website: www.lancasterrefugees.org

Church World Service Offices Worldwide —

Church World Service - Africa
P.O. Box 14176-00800, Nairobi, Kenya
Phone: +254 20 444 2204 / 0652; Fax: +254 20 445 6066
Email: info@cwsea.org
Website: www.cwsafrica.org

Church World Service - Asia/Pacific
10th Floor, CCT Building, 328 Phayathai Road
Ratchathewi, Bangkok 10400, Thailand
Phone: +66 (0)2 214 6077; Fax: +66 (0)2 214 6078
Website: www.cwsasiapacific.org

Church World Service - Cambodia
43, Street 112, Sangkat Phsar Depou Ti Bei

Khan Tuol Kouk, Phnom Penh, Cambodia
Phone: +855 23 881 912
Information: info@cwscambodia.org
Website: www.cwscambodia.org

Church World Service - Indonesia
Jl. Ampera Raya No. 5A, DKI Jakarta 12560
Phone: +62-21-78838437; Fax: +62-21-7804284
Information: info@cwsindonesia.or.id
Website: www.cwsindonesia.or.id/en/

Church World Service - Laos
Box 820, Vientiane, Lao PDR
Phone: +856-21-212785; Fax: +856-21-27878

Church World Service - Pakistan/Afghanistan
P.O. Box #20048, Karachi, Pakistan
Phone: +92-21-439-0541; Fax: +92-21-439-0922
Email: cwspa@cyber.net.pk
Website: www.cwspa.org

Church World Service - Vietnam
I.P.O Box 176, Hanoi, Vietnam
Phone: +84-4-3-8328 569; Fax: +84-4-3-8328 629
Email: cws@cws.org.vn
Website: www.cws.org.vn/html/home.htm

Church World Service - Europe Min Office
Dorda Stanojevica 11/70, Belgrade, 11070, Serbia
Phone: +381-11-6300310

CWS Min Office - Latin America and the Caribbean
Camacuá 238-B
(1406) Buenos Aires, Argentina
Phone/Fax: +5411-4633-0833
Email: info@cwslac.org
Website: www.cwslac.org
800-297-1516 or 574-264-3102

OTHER RESETTLEMENT AGENCIES —

World Relief Corporation (WR) – Website: www.wr.org
Online eBook – *Volunteer Resource Guide: A Handbook for Volunteers Working with Refugees in Tucson, Arizona*
Website: www.iskashitaa.org/Portals/1/Downloads/Vol_resource_TRG%20Manual%20FINAL6_2010.pdf

U.S. Committee for Refugees and Immigrants (USCRI)
Address: 2231 Crystal Drive, Suite 350, Arlington, VA 22202-3794
Phone: 703-310-1130 • fax: 703-769-4241
Website: www.refugees.org

Catholic World Relief: 'CARITAS' Refugee Resettlement
Address: 2050 Ballenger Avenue, Suite 400, Alexandria, VA 22314
Phone: 703-549-1390
Website: www.caritas.org/what-we-do/migration

Catholic: BRYCS, a.k.a., "Bridging Refugee Youth and Children's Services"
Address: United States Conference of Catholic Bishops,
3211 Fourth Street NE, Washington, DC 20017
Phone: 1-888-572-6500
Website: www.brycs.org/aboutRefugees/refugee101.cfm
Website: www.brycs.org/publications

Christian Reformed Church, Office of Social Justice.
Website: www2.crcna.org/pages/osj_immigrationreform.cfm

Episcopal Church, USA – Refugee Resettlement
www.ecusa.anglican.org/emm
Website:http://library.episcopalchurch.org/sites/default/files/central_american_migrants_an_episcopal_response_webinar_slides.pdf

Episcopal Migration Ministries (EMM)
Website: www.episcopalmigrationministries.org/

Ethiopian Community Development Council (ECDC)
Website: www.ecdcinternational.org

Hebrew Immigrant Aid Society (HIAS)
Website: www.hias.org/work/resettling-refugees and www.hias.org/refugee-assistance-oranizationshias-partners

International Institute of Minnesota
    Website: http://www.iimn.org/services/refugee-resettlement

International Rescue Committee (IRC)
    Website: www.theirc.org

Iowa, Bureau of Refugee Services
    Website: www.dhs.state.ia.us/refugee

Lutheran Immigration and Refugee Services (LIRS)
    Website: www.lirs.org

Lutheran Resettlement and Immigration Services
    Website: http://lirs.org/our-work/partnership/service-partners/
    refugee-resettlement-partners

Lutheran Immigration and Refugee Service
    Phone: (410) 230-2757
    Websites: www.lirs.org/fostercare; www.fosterparentinfo@lirs.org

Lutheran Social Services of the Southwest
    Website: www.refugeefocus.org/wp-content/uploads/2013/01/Volunteer-
    Handbook.pdf

Mennonite Church, USA
    Website: http://mcc.org/learn/what/categories/immigration

Mennonite Church, Canada
    Website: http://mcc.org/learn/what/categories/immigration

Minnesota Council of Churches - Director of Refugee Services
    Phone: (612) 874-8605
    Website: www.mnchurches.org/refugeeservices

Orthodox Church
    Website: www.refugees.org/our-work/refugee-resettlement

United Church of Christ
    Website: www.ucc.org/refugees
    Phone: 866-822-8224 (toll free) ext. 3212

U.S. Conference of Catholic Bishops
    3211 Fourth Street NE, Washington, DC 20017

Phone: (888) 572-6500
Website: www.brycs.org/aboutRefugees/refugee101.cfm

U.S. Conference of Catholic Bishops (foster care for refugee children)
Website: www.usccb.org and www.migratingchildren@usccb.org
Phone: (202) 541-3081

Voluntary Resettlement Agencies (VOLAGs)
"Overview of resettlement agencies/responsibilities"
Website:www.dss.cahwnet.gov/refugeeprogram/res/pdf/Factsheets/
VOLAGs_FactSheet.pdf

World Relief: National Association of Evangelicals
Website: https://worldrelief.org/refugee-resettlement
Contact: Jenny Yang; eMail: jyang@wr.org
Phone: (443) 527-8363

OTHER RECOMMENDED RESOURCES

IAN (Immigration Advocates, Nonprofit Resource Center)
Resources for non-profit advocates, organizers, and service providers for refugees. Supported by Bill and Melinda Gates Foundation and other philanthropic organizations. Website: www.immigrationadvocates.org/nonprofit

"Five Ways to Stand Up and Be the Church in the World's Worst Refugee Crisis Since World War II" Author: Anne Voskamp
Website: www.aholyexperience.com/2015/09/5-ways-to-stand-up-be-the-church-in-the-worlds-worst-refugee-crisis-since-world-war-ii

Office of Refugee Resettlement & Refugee Health Key Resources
Refugee health newsletters; culturally/linguistically targeted refugee women's health videos; emergency preparedness booklet
Website: www.acf.hhs.gov/programs/orr/programs/refugee-health

Health Insurance for Refugees:
Culturally/linguistically targeted videos on health insurance, refugees, & more – Website: www.acf.hhs.gov/programs/orr/health

Office of Refugee Resettlement & Ethnic Community Self Help:
Website: www.acf.hhs.gov/programs/orr/programs/ethnic-community-self-help

"First Steps: An LIRS Guide for Refugees, Asylum Seekers and Migrants Released from Detention" (book). Lutheran Immigration and Refugee Service, 2014. This is a practical resource covering reunification of families, green cards, becoming a U.S. citizen, employment, health care, education, emotional support, religious support groups, legal services, etc.

"Foster Care for UnaccompaniedChildren from Central America"
Website: http://oca.org/resource-handbook/commservice/helping-to-resettle-refugees

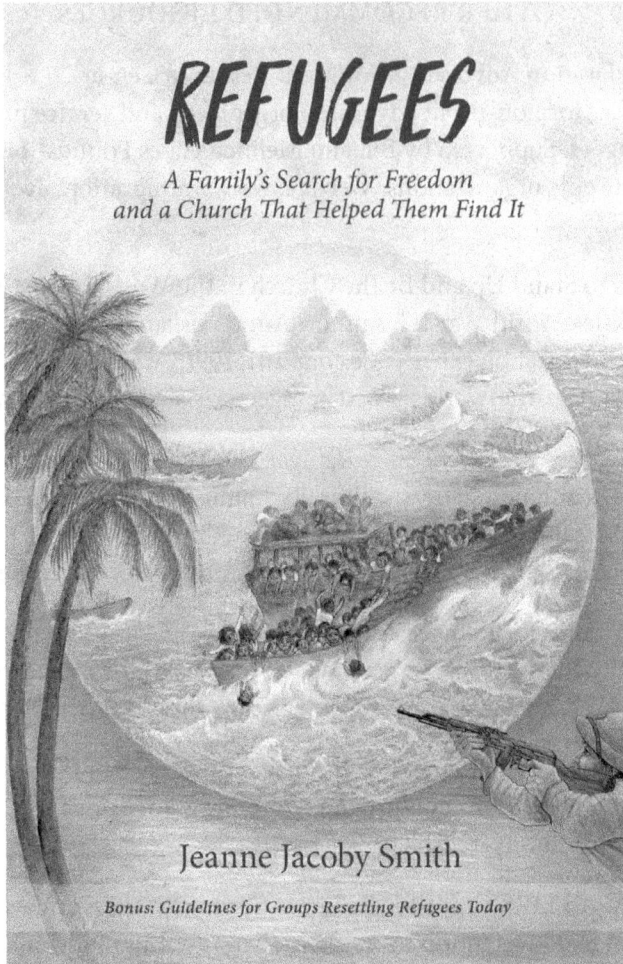

BOOK ORDERS FOR
*Refugees: A Family's Search for Freedom
and a Church That Helped Them Find It*
by Jeanne Jacoby Smith

Orders taken at:
www.Amazon.com — paperback
www.kindle.com — ebook for Kindle

www.ingramcontent.com/pod-product-compliance
Lightning Source LLC
Chambersburg PA
CBHW060846280326
41934CB00007B/937